INDIE AUTHOR CONFIDENTIAL

SECRETS NO ONE WILL TELL YOU ABOUT BEING A WRITER, VOL 11.

M.L. RONN

CONTENTS

About This Series   v
Introduction   vii

BECOME A WORLD-CLASS
CONTENT CREATOR

Using Stock Photos at Speaking Engagements   3
Writing One Million Words Per Year   5
More Improvements to My Editing Workflow   9
Doing the Ray Bradbury Challenge
Retroactively   11
Getting Back into Short Stories   13
Writing Flash Fiction and Microfiction   17
Collaboration 2.0   21
The Ultimate Writing Challenge   23
Lessons in Setting   27
Writing an Idea While It's Hot   31

BECOME A TECHNOLOGY AND
DATA-DRIVEN WRITER

Building a Word Count Tracker   35
Lessons in Cover Design This Quarter   37
Experiments with AI-Generated Art   39
More Math Behind Cover Design   45
Book Preview App   49
Additional Thoughts on Sales Tracking for
Authors   51
Stream Deck Revisited   55
Upgrading My Microphone   59

Whisper: A Watershed Moment in AI Transcription   63

The Power of Digital Highlighters   69

The Case for a Writing Computer Not Connected to the Internet   73

Hotel Libraries and Little Free Libraries   79

LOOKING FORWARD

Dealing with a Productivity Slump   85

Dealing with Economic Downturns   89

Designing New Business Cards   93

The Return to Microsoft Word   95

Traveling to Saudi Arabia   97

Kickstarter Lessons   103

Audio Commentary Revisited   105

Writing While Traveling   109

Self-Sufficient Self-Publishing   113

My Thoughts on The Metaverse   121

Mastering the Fundamentals   129

Q4 Progress Report   133

My 2023 Strategic Priorities   137

Can You Keep a Secret?   139

Meet M.L. Ronn   141

More Books by M.L. Ronn   143

ABOUT THIS SERIES

This isn't your typical writing self-help book. This series is a compilation of lessons learned from an indie author trying to walk the path to success. Follow author M.L. Ronn (Michael La Ronn) as he navigates what it means to master the craft of writing, marketing, and running a profitable publishing business. Learn from his successes and failures, and learn about things that most successful authors only talk about behind the scenes.

INTRODUCTION

Here we are at the end of another year. Honestly, I'm glad to see the end of 2022. My introduction will be thin this quarter.

My Core Strategic Priorities

As a refresher, my mission is to create content that entertains and/or educates my audience, preferably both, and to remain nimble in an ever-changing industry. I do this by focusing on three strategic priorities:

- Become a world-class content creator
- Become a technology and data-driven writer
- Become the writer of the future (looking forward)

What's in This Volume

In the World-Class Content Creator section, I discuss my return to short fiction and how it will help me build my platform.

In the Technology and Data-Driven Writer section, I

discuss lessons in cover design, upgrading my audiovisual setup for my YouTube channel and interviews, and a powerful new transcription tool that could change the way I dictate.

In the Looking Forward section, I share thoughts about economic downturns, a once-in-a-lifetime trip to Saudi Arabia, and my thoughts on mastering the fundamentals.

Enjoy this volume.

—M.L. Ronn
December 23, 2022
Des Moines, Iowa

BECOME A WORLD-CLASS CONTENT CREATOR

USING STOCK PHOTOS AT SPEAKING ENGAGEMENTS

I am always cautious about the graphics I use.

Early in my career, I frequently used images from the public domain or the Creative Commons. I (mistakenly) thought that because these images were allowed to be used for free and commercial use, I would be covered.

I was wrong.

As I learned more about copyright and protecting the creative works of others, I realized that relying on Creative Commons and public domain work was unwise.

First, you have no way of knowing whether an artist has created that work or if they have stolen it. If an image is removed from a Creative Commons search engine due to theft or a copyright infringement allegation, you don't know about it unless you happen to look up that image one day and discover that it's gone...or you get sued.

Therefore, I no longer use Creative Commons images or anything public domain in my books or marketing. It's just bad business.

I have switched to using paid stock media instead. It is not cheap, and you can't always find what you're looking for, but you don't have to worry about copyright infringement or theft (for the most part). This is because stock media sites do a good job of policing their content. Many also offer a liability guarantee so that if you are accused of copyright infringement when using an image from their site, they will step in and defend you. Also, if you can produce a license from a stock media site, you're probably not going to be sued anyway.

I did a speaking event that required visual aids. Normally, I do not like to put images in my presentations. It makes everything easier because the organizer doesn't have to worry about where the images came from. For this particular event, I decided to do something different. Once I built the presentation, I purchased all the necessary licenses. Then, I downloaded each license (which has my name, the date purchased, a small thumbnail of the image, the image asset ID number, and a stamp of authenticity). I then built a table in a Microsoft Word document that listed the slide number, a description of the image, and a link to the image on the stock media site where I purchased it. Every slide had a corresponding entry on the table. When I sent my slide deck to the organizer, I included the Word document with the table and a link to a Google Drive folder that contained copies of all the licenses I purchased. I made it very easy for the organizer to do their due diligence on my due diligence.

The organizer was impressed with my documentation and fast-tracked my presentation for approval. I have a hunch that the company's attorneys also looked at this document because the organizer said their legal department appreciated my attention to detail.

This was an incredibly successful exercise that I will duplicate whenever I want to use visuals in my presentations. I still won't use visuals unless I have to, but it's good to have a process in place that will protect the organizer and me if I do.

WRITING ONE MILLION WORDS PER YEAR

Now that I have improved my writing process workflow and can consistently achieve between 3,000 and 5,000 words daily, it's time to take my planning to the next level.

I have always wanted to achieve pulp-level productivity. I have always been intrigued by how the old pulp writers wrote millions of words per year nonstop.

I have written many times in this series about how I admire prolific personalities. I gravitate toward them because they possess a skill that I also have and want to perfect. When I study the lives of prolific personalities, I feel as if I have unlocked something within myself.

Therefore, I am ready to try something different. I have consistently written between 500,000 and 600,000 words for the last eight years. Depending on the books I wrote, this equated to somewhere between 8 and 12 books per year. The average is eight. I have been happy with that number, and while it has given me an amazing portfolio, I know I can do better.

The next level for me is one million words per year. This equates to 2,750 words per day, 21,000 words per week, and 84,000 words per month.

This is a tough, tough word count goal to achieve, but it only represents the minimum level of what the old pulp writers could do. Imagine a career with a writer writing several million words each year without missing. When I think about that, I think about all the new worlds, characters, and lessons I could meet. It's an endless journey on which there is no destination. I find that fascinating.

So, I will try to write one million words in 2023.

It's not as easy as simply sitting down to write and hoping for the best. It requires a surprising amount of planning and foresight. For example, you have to be able to tell one story right after the other. Most authors I know like to have a "recharge" after they finish a book. They view finishing a book as a monumental challenge worthy of celebration and rest. There is no doing such a thing when you want to write at pulp speed. Because of the math, you literally cannot take a break.

To write one story after the other, you always have to know what to write next. What do you write? How do you determine what to write next? When you start writing *really* fast, you realize just how deep your creative well needs to be to sustain such a fast, consistent pace. This is not for the faint of heart.

My biggest challenge in writing one million words has been twofold.

First, I have had to systematize what I write next. I now must know what I will write at least *two* books in advance. This way, I always know what's next when I finish a book. Also, my daily word quota minimum is 2,750 words per day. This means that if I finish a book and I am at 2,000 words for the day, I must find 750 additional words, which means I need to start another project right away, often immediately after I type "The End." That takes guts and a complete elimination of fear to pull off.

The second challenge is dealing with bottlenecks. For example, once I have finished a book, I have to review it one more time to ensure everything is good to go. You know me well enough by now to know that I write my books in one draft on a first-time final basis. I focus on getting the story right the first time so that I don't have to worry about revision. That said, I make a "final pass" through the story, looking for any last-minute typos and plot holes that need to be fixed. This is a brisk run through the book, and it doesn't take much time (usually a day or two in addition to all of my other responsibilities), but it does require time, which eats away at my writing time. Because this doesn't take too long, I have been willing to sacrifice a little writing time to get books to my editor promptly. I usually try to make up for any deficiencies in my quota over the next few days.

There's also the bottleneck of publishing. It takes time to format and publish a book too. I also am willing to sacrifice a little writing time to publish new books because, obviously, that is one of the best things I can do to further my career. But it does create a bottleneck.

When you write at pulp speed, you must keep things moving at a steady clip. You've got to keep your projects moving forward every day. Otherwise, you will fall off the wagon. And once you fall off, the math gets brutal.

I am turning to short stories to help me regulate my flow. Short stories are helpful because if I'm not ready to write the next book, I can write a short story. For example, if I want to write a book that will require some research, I can't just dive into it, but I have to keep things moving somehow. I can write short stories while researching this book and maintain my word count.

Writing one million words in a year is an amazing accomplishment and one that I look forward to celebrating and sustaining for many years to come.

MORE IMPROVEMENTS TO MY EDITING WORKFLOW

I received edits for several books this quarter after making enhancements to my dictation and editing workflow. While the results were outstanding, I noticed a few things I wasn't happy about.

For starters, introducing a voice recorder into my workflow exploded my word counts and improved my transcription accuracy, but I did notice an uptick in errors flagged by my editor. Many of these issues were silly issues that would have never existed if I had typed the book, like confused homonyms or nonsensical words.

Now, I review my manuscripts very carefully before sending them to my editor, but I can't catch everything. That's why I use a copyeditor and proofreader!

I kept asking myself if I could do better. I truly believe that no tools on the market can help me further reduce my errors. I find it to be an interesting contradiction of our time that there are AI tools that can write compelling chapters in books with no typos, yet the best AI editors on the market still don't know the difference between the words "two" and "too." I don't understand that.

Anyway, I found myself revisiting Grammarly Premium. I wanted to see if it could help me catch more dictation-related errors.

Grammarly Premium has come a long way. Not only did it help me catch more dictation-related errors, but it also helped me catch more errors.

The only problem? It also produced more false positives. However, if I waded through the results, I liked what I saw.

So, I purchased Grammarly Premium and am now using that to help me produce cleaner manuscripts.

Next, I took advantage of Microsoft Word's Read Aloud feature, which reads your text to you. I have found this to be a vital way of spotting dictation-related errors because I can often hear problems that my eyes miss. For example, if I edit exclusively by staring at a computer screen, my eyes get tired, and I will eventually start to miss things. However, if I stare at the screen while also listening to the text, I find many more errors that become harder to miss. My ears do a lot of the heavy lifting, allowing me to edit for longer before getting tired.

Also, I have found that Read Aloud helps me get through chapters faster because it helps me move at a quick, measured pace. I discovered that it takes me three minutes on average to review a page while listening to Read Aloud. I have no idea how long it would take me if I were editing manually, but I suspect it would be longer than three minutes. This gives me a predictable workflow. I know that it will take me three minutes per page to edit. When you consider that I already produce clean text through my dictation methods, and I already use tools like Word's Editor, Grammarly, ProWritingAid, and PerfectIt to clean the text even further, Read Aloud helps me regulate my editing speed.

Anyway, I continue to refine my editing workflow to achieve world-class writing and editing speeds.

DOING THE RAY BRADBURY
CHALLENGE RETROACTIVELY

I've always wanted to do the Ray Bradbury Challenge. Well, *both* Ray Bradbury challenges.

Ray Bradbury was the writer who inspired me to sit down at the keyboard and become a professional writer. He was a once-in-a-civilization talent. If I can even be as half as successful as he was, I will be somebody.

Ray Bradbury offered two challenges to new writers to help them improve their craft and further their careers.

The first challenge, which is deceptively difficult, is to read one short story, one poem, and one essay every day for 365 days. This will fill your creative well and keep you inspired.

The *concept* of the first challenge is simple, but the devil is in the details. For example, how do you find a short story, poem, and essay to read every day? Believe it or not, that requires a lot of planning. Do you read the works of one author per category, or do you randomize them?

Anyway, the first challenge is not hard, but it is time-consuming.

The second challenge is the most famous. In that challenge, Bradbury recommends writing one short story per week for a year. This will result in 52 short stories. To paraphrase Ray Bradbury, you can write 52 short stories, but it is impossible to write 52 bad short stories. They can't be all bad. And the really good ones might just change your career.

I've always had the second challenge in my sights. This quarter, I began writing more short stories professionally. My goal is to try to get stories published in professional magazines. This requires organization, discipline, and a whole lot of effort.

I wrote two short stories in one week and had a couple of ideas:

- What if I did the Ray Bradbury Challenge?
- What if, instead of doing a short story per week, I focused on 52 short stories in a year? This would free me from the weekly requirement, but I would still be required to write 52 short stories in a year.
- What if I started the Bradbury challenge *now* instead of waiting for January 1?

I was intrigued.

So, I'm doing the Ray Bradbury Challenge now. Will I be successful? I have no idea. However, the way I see it, if I fail, I will still have a lot of short stories to show for it, and some of those stories might even be accepted by a magazine.

In other words, I have absolutely nothing to lose.

GETTING BACK INTO SHORT STORIES

Last quarter, a mentor challenged me to reconsider writing short stories. As I discussed in the previous volume, I love short stories, but I have found it mentally difficult to write them in recent years because I am so focused on novels. My mentor challenged me to break that mindset.

Here's how I did it.

First, I adopted the Lester Dent plot formula method of telling stories. This step-by-step method does an excellent job of helping you hit all the elements you need to write an engaging short story that magazine editors will buy.

Dent was a pulp writer. I consider myself to be styled after the pulp writers. It's how I see the world, so I've always gravitated toward this method. I've used the Dent method in the past, but this time, I wanted to truly master it. Every story I have written this year has followed the method almost to a T. When I deviated from it, I had a good reason to do so.

The Lester Dent plot formula assumes a 6,000-word short story. You take it and divide the story into 1,500-word increments. Each increment has a beat, resulting in a steady cadence that readers have come to expect over the years.

Next, I read a lot of short stories.

Then, I developed a system to help me get organized with my short stories. If I do the Ray Bradbury Challenge, it means that I am going to have dozens of short stories. If I'm going to do all that work, it doesn't make sense for those stories to sit on my computer, so I have to push them out to magazines. Therein lies the trouble.

Using the Master Publishing File spreadsheet I created last year to help me track my intellectual property, I added a tab for short stories. This way, I could inventory my short stories and record the title, length, genre, and associated keywords with the story, such as love, coming-of-age, the 1970s, and more—helpful when reviewing anthologies with themes, for example. This gave me a good sense of what I had in my portfolio currently, and how to build my portfolio strategically with future stories.

Next, after I inventoried my work and built a scalable way to capture future work quickly, I added another tab on my Master Publishing File spreadsheet that listed the title of the story and magazine information. For example, if I submit a story to Magazine X, then I need to keep a record of that. I don't care about dates, but I do need to know *where* I have sent stories. In my experience, tracking dates is depressing and not at all worth doing, so I'm not going to do it.

I also captured how long it takes for the pro markets to return one of my stories. Most decide on stories within 30 to 90 days.

Also, there are dozens of magazines that I could submit a story to if I wanted. I counted at least 50. Some are professional markets; some are semipro; others don't pay anything.

While I want to gather as many readers as I can, I had to decide on how to proceed here. On the one hand, you want to send stories out to as many magazines as possible; on the other hand, sending your story to *every* magazine will take *years* until you know whether it is accepted or rejected. During that time, your story is "locked up," and you can't do anything with it.

If you publish a story, you can no longer publish it in a magazine, as magazines don't reprint self-published work.

Like I said, it's a delicate balance.

Here are the criteria I landed on:

1. I will only submit my stories to professional (read: paying) magazine markets that accept science fiction and fantasy stories. If I happen to write something in another genre, I will consider other magazines on a case-by-case basis.
2. The average paying market takes between 30 and 90 days to make a decision. I will allow a story to surf the markets for at least one year or until it receives an acceptance, whichever is less.
3. If a story is accepted, I will diary one year and attempt to get the story reprinted in *another* magazine that accepts reprints to maximize my copyright licensing. The story will also go into my next short story collection, since the rights will have reverted to me within a short time period.
4. If a story is not accepted (or if one year expires from the first day of submission), I will publish it in my next short story collection.

We'll see how this goes. At the time of this writing, I have five stories out for magazine consideration. I'm intrigued by what it will look like if I complete the Ray Bradbury Challenge and have dozens of stories floating around out there.

I'm going to find out whether Ray Bradbury's advice was right!

WRITING FLASH FICTION AND MICROFICTION

I want to be a great practitioner of the fiction craft.

Fiction means many things:

- novels
- novellas
- short stories
- flash fiction
- microfiction

Generally, a novel is considered anything greater than 40,000 words, and microfiction is anything less than 100 words. You can even subdivide microfiction further, but I think that's a bit much.

That said, if I want to consider myself a practitioner of fiction, I should be a practitioner of *fiction*. This means writing it in every form. Doing so gives me perspective, improves my imagination, and helps me hone skills that I would never otherwise hone if I were just writing novels.

That's why I've been thinking a lot lately about diversifying my portfolio with short fiction. The great thing about short fiction is that you can write it quickly (especially in my case), and it is a great marketing tool. It is a wonderful way to introduce new readers to your work. It doesn't cost anything except the time you take to write it. If you write quickly like I do, we're talking a matter of hours. If you sell a 5,000-word short story to a magazine at a professional rate of eight cents per word, you will make $400. Hell, you might publish a novel and not make anywhere near that. You'd have to sell approximately 115 copies of a novel to make that much money at $4.99 with a 70 percent sales commission.

The math is lucrative with short fiction, but you must be willing to do the work and be organized.

When I was in New York City earlier this year, I met Ran Walker, a fellow author who specializes in flash and microfiction. Ran has a sizable bibliography of published works in magazines, and he frequently speaks on this art form. I chatted with him about his approach and filed his advice for when I needed it someday. It appears that day has arrived.

Flash fiction is simple to write, but that doesn't make it easy. If I do the math, I could be a pretty prolific flash fiction writer if I wanted to be. When I walk my dog, I dictate at least 500 words every session. I walk my dog at least three times a day, sometimes more if I want good exercise. That's 1,500 words per day, or the equivalent of a flash fiction piece. In one day.

That's just the time I spend walking my dog. When I factor in the time I spend driving, doing chores like dishes and laundry, and the good ol' time I spend in front of the computer typing, I could probably write two to three flash fiction pieces in a single day if I was inspired, with plenty of room left over.

What would my career look like if I built a solid body of novels and novellas, short stories, flash fiction, and microfiction? How much flash fiction and microfiction would I need to write to be considered prolific?

It's hard to know for sure, but I think the answer is *at least* 100 pieces. I don't know any speculative fiction writers who have written that much. Therefore, that is a good number to shoot for—100 pieces with an average of 700 words per piece would be approximately 70,000 words, which is a long novel.

Sure, I could do that.

As I think about ways to accomplish my goal of one million words (minimum) in 2023, I consider flash fiction and microfiction to be two more tools in my toolbox.

COLLABORATION 2.0

While at the annual Writer's Digest Conference in New York City, I had the opportunity to meet and spend time with Matty Dalrymple, fellow author and podcast host of the "Indy Author Podcast." I have been on Matty's show many times, and it was great to meet her in person.

We got along famously, and we did a recap of the event on a subsequent episode of her podcast after returning home. The topic was how to get the most out of in-person speaking events, and we both talked about our experiences as professional public speakers. After the show, I made an offhand remark that the topic we discussed would make a great book. She asked if I was interested in collaborating on one. I said yes.

Over the next 24 hours, we developed a plan to write a book on how authors can master public speaking. The concept focused on the business and logistic sides of speaking rather than the rhetorical part.

Matty and I are on the same page regarding how we see writing and business, so the first thing we did was draft a contract between us that clearly outlined the responsibilities of each party, who would publish the book, how royalties would be split, and so on. We agreed to split the royalties through Draft2Digital's Payment Split service, which makes everything easier. We also built in contingencies for what happens when one of us dies or becomes incapacitated. A key provision of the contract explicitly indicated that, in the event of death or incapacitation of one of the parties, the other automatically has the right to unpublish the book and republish under their own publishing company. This will help considerably with retailer conversations.

I used some other lessons I picked up in *The Author Estate Handbook*, plus some more great ideas from Matty. The result was a contract that ensured we were in agreement before beginning. After all, this is a permanent business endeavor. It's not something to embark on lightly.

We executed the contract through an online contract signing service.

We outlined the book using Google Sheets, with each person taking their share of chapters.

We also did extensive market research, determining where the book fit in the market, who our target readers were, and how to attract them. Two heads were definitely better than one.

We decided on the style of the book and how it would be written—with a blended author voice that reflected both Matty's and mine.

We coauthored the book in Google Docs, developing a system for writing and suggesting comments.

The book is still in production, and I look forward to discussing it further in the next volume of this series, but it feels good to collaborate with someone again. It is so much easier now than it was in 2016. The tools have gotten much better.

THE ULTIMATE WRITING CHALLENGE

I've been thinking about ways to push my writing productivity to the next level.

In the writing community, there is no shortage of "challenges." These challenges are designed to help writers reach the next level of their careers.

That got me thinking about a challenge for intermediate and advanced writers that would turn them into a writer's writer.

I present "The Ultimate Writing Challenge." It's four challenges in one, and you must do all of them in one year.

CHALLENGE #1: WRITE ONE MILLION WORDS

I've talked enough about writing one million words in this series, but to recap, it means you must write at least 2,750 words per day, 19,236 words per week, and 84,000 words per month. This is a lot of words.

CHALLENGE #2: WRITE 12 NOVELS

In other words, write one novel per month, or, do the NaNoWriMo challenge each month.

Every November, writers worldwide try to write a novel in 30 days. For 99 percent of these writers, it is an annual event. With the Ultimate Writing Challenge, every month is NaNoWriMo!

CHALLENGE #3: WRITE 52 SHORT STORIES

The great writer Ray Bradbury recommended writing 52 short stories in a year because he believed that it was impossible to write 52 bad short stories in a row. They can't be all bad. I agree.

Add in the Ray Bradbury Challenge in addition to NaNoWriMo, and you have a compelling and difficult goal.

The next and final part of the challenge is the real doozy...

CHALLENGE #4: ADHERE TO HEINLEIN'S RULES

Robert Heinlein was a golden-age science fiction writer who laid out five simple business rules for writers. The rules are:

1. You must write.
2. You must finish what you write.
3. You must not rewrite, except to editorial demand.
4. You must put your work on the market.
5. You must keep your work on the market until sold.

Writing and finishing your work is not a big deal for most writers once they have a few novels under their belt, but the last three rules are brutal.

First, I believe Heinlein's rule about revising is a good one:

don't rewrite your work unless the editor tells you to. If you write novels and submit them to traditional publishers, then you shouldn't rewrite them unless an editor recommends it. If you write short stories and submit them to magazines, you should not rewrite unless the magazine editor requires it. In short, you must learn to write your books in one draft, and cleanly. This is the place in Heinlein's Rules that most writers check out.

And we haven't even gotten to publishing yet!

If we adjust Heinlein's Rules to reflect the era of indie publishing, we could say this:

- For novels, you must self-publish them or always keep them out for consideration by publishers and agents.
- If you write short stories, you must send them to magazines until sold and/or self-publish them.

For short stories, you could do a hybrid, submitting your stories to markets for a limited period of time (say one year) and then self-publishing if you receive no acceptances.

Whatever you do, you must keep your work out there so that a rights buyer can license it or readers can buy it.

The Heinlein's Rules part of this challenge makes it almost impossible for most people.

BRINGING IT ALL TOGETHER

To recap the Ultimate Writing Challenge, you must:

1. Write one million words in one year.
2. Write 12 novels
3. Write 52 short stories
4. Adhere to Heinlein's rules

Boy, is this a tough challenge, but consider the benefits.

In just one year, you will have written more novels and short stories than almost all writers working currently. To quantify this, you will write and publish at least 64 pieces of intellectual property (novels and short stories). That's a big deal.

Quality-wise, I can't guarantee that you will be a better writer, but I'm pretty sure that you will be. All you have to do is compare your first short story and novel to your last. I think the difference would be astounding.

Next, if you receive an acceptance in a short story magazine or publish a book that takes off, that will be its own reward. You will level up.

Those are just a few of the benefits I can think of. Complete the Ultimate Writing Challenge, and you will be well on your way to becoming a world-class writer in no time.

LESSONS IN SETTING

Earlier this year, I entered the Writers of the Future contest. It is a free contest that writers can enter for cash prizes and potential entry into the *Writers of the Future* anthology. Many household science fiction and fantasy writers that you know and love were previous contest winners, such as Patrick Rothfuss. The contest is a proving ground for burgeoning speculative fiction writers.

I have nothing to lose from submitting, so I send a story to the contest each quarter. My very first entry earned me a Silver Honorable Mention, which is one step away from Semifinalist, which means that I could have possibly been featured in the anthology. In other words, it's the highest level achievable without winning. Pretty cool and pretty encouraging.

I sent the story to one of my mentors for feedback. This person has been a judge in major contests and understands the psychology of someone reviewing slush piles. I asked him where the story potentially went wrong and what I could work on for the next story. (Please note: I asked him for feedback on the story, not so that I could fix it, but so that I could fix the problem in my next story. I don't believe in revising or rewriting.)

My mentor told me I had a great opening, but my setting wasn't strong enough. To paraphrase him, he told me it felt like my characters were in a white room talking and taking action, but the reader couldn't see the actions unfold because the setting was weak.

That was hard advice to hear because I have taken great strides over the past few years to make sure that I describe settings through the eyes of my viewpoint character, and in the five senses. I believe that I am doing this well most of the time, but this time, I didn't. It made me rethink how I approach this writing tactic. It also made me recommit to it so that I never make this mistake again. Honestly, the advice was a bit embarrassing and humbling.

When I want to learn anything new, I study the mega bestsellers: John Grisham, Nora Roberts, James Patterson, and so on. I studied ten openings by three authors, writing down the commonalities of each. I only paid attention to how the authors did their settings. It was eye-opening. I discovered with all three authors that they practice a technique best described as "winding up" the setting.

For example, they will start a chapter almost exclusively with setting through the eyes of the viewpoint character, described in the five senses. If you look at the first 500 words of the story and color-code the sections where setting is described, you will see a common pattern. First, you will notice that the descriptions of setting are most dense at the beginning of the chapter and become less frequent as the opening continues. This is when the author is "winding up" the setting. They give the reader tons of information to help them see the story and characters. Once the reader has enough information, the author backs off a little, describing the setting less frequently (but still describing the setting).

This begs two questions:

1. How much does it take to "wind up" a setting?
2. How much is enough (and by proxy, how much is too little and too much?)

When I study the mega bestsellers, I like to color-code the text. I will highlight the words associated with the technique I'm studying. This allows me to see their techniques better.

Here are my observations:

- All three mega bestsellers wound up their settings within the first 500 words of a chapter. In each of these chapters, setting descriptions accounted for between 50 and 75 percent of all words on the page.
- Immediately after the first 500 words, the setting became approximately 10 to 20 percent of all words on the page.
- The author began winding up again whenever there was a new setting, new chapter or section break, or turn of events.

In other words, the authors wound up the setting, let it go until they felt the readers needed more information, and once the wind-up ran out, they began the process again.

I committed to following this same technique in my stories. Hopefully, I will never receive feedback on poor settings again.

WRITING AN IDEA WHILE IT'S HOT

I set myself up for trouble this quarter. I did something I knew I shouldn't have done, but I did it anyway because I thought I could overcome it. I started a short story before I knew I had to take a writing break.

My wife was scheduled to go out of town on Tuesday. I started a short story on Monday night. Big mistake.

The story started off fine enough. I had a good sense of the character, setting, and plot. However, I truly had to take time away from my writing while my wife was out of town because I had to care for my daughter, pets, and house.

Here's what happened:

- I wrote the first 1,000 words of the story.
- I took a five-day break, and when I returned to the writing desk, I had lost the energy for the story.
- It took me almost two weeks to finish the damn story.
- I eventually found the energy, and I'm happy with how the story turned out, all things considered, but it took way too long.

Here's what I should have done: I shouldn't have written the story. I should have found some other project to commit words to that wouldn't have resulted in a loss of energy. Doing so would have allowed me to step away from my writing and return with a clean slate.

Instead, I got a great idea and wrote it, thinking that I could overcome this when I should have known better.

Oh well. You live and you learn. I still followed Heinlein's Rules. I started the story. I finished it. And I submitted it to literary magazines. That's what matters. But if I want to write one million words per year, I can't afford to make these types of mistakes again.

BECOME A TECHNOLOGY AND DATA-DRIVEN WRITER

BUILDING A WORD COUNT TRACKER

In my quest to write one million words each year, I need a tool to help me stay organized. Otherwise, I won't know how many words I've written and how many words I need to write to achieve my goal.

Here's the problem: most specialized writing apps allow you to track your words per project by day, week, and month. That's great, but no writing app I know of (other than Atticus) allows you to track your word counts across multiple projects. For example, if I divide my daily word count between Project A and Project B, in most writing apps, I have to check my statistics in each project individually and then add them together. That's no good.

Instead, I need a global word count tracker that tracks these numbers. This is important because I sometimes work on more than one project in a day, especially if I finish one book and launch into another right away. Often, I will finish a book and start a new one on the same day. Not being able to get a word count on all the projects I've worked on every day is inefficient.

Instead, I relied on good old Microsoft Excel.

I developed a tracker in Microsoft Excel that tells me in

real-time how many words I've written, how many I have left ago, and some other metrics to help me understand how I am performing.

First, I have a plan of 1,252,000 words between August 28, 2022, and August 28, 2023. Because I didn't start my year on January 1, the plan number is a little weird.

Next, I keep track of my surplus and deficit. For example, if I need to write 2,750 words per day, if I write 3,000 words, I have a surplus of 250 words for the day; if I write 2,000 words, I have a deficit of 750 words. If I'm ahead, I technically need to write fewer words the next day to stay on track. If I'm behind, I will need to write more words to catch up. Since my quota is 2,750 words per day, a day's productivity is worth that much. I wrote a formula to express how many "days" ahead or behind I am. The tracker also shows me my average word count.

At the end of each day, I update the tracker and check my progress. So far, I am operating at a good surplus this year. I am approximately 30,000 words ahead of schedule at the time of this writing, representing somewhere around 13 days ahead. That's a great place to be in case I get sick or need to take some time off. I can miss up to 13 days and still hit my plan for the year! That's the power of knowing your numbers.

That said, I don't want to rest on my laurels. Every day I can, I write more than 2,750 words. Sometimes, I only write a few hundred extra words. Other times, I write several thousand extra words. Building a strong surplus helped me weather this challenge.

The word count tracker has become an indispensable tool to help me achieve my goals.

LESSONS IN COVER DESIGN THIS QUARTER

I have finally put my money where my mouth is. I made substantial progress in designing my own book covers this quarter. In fact, I made such significant progress that I am astounded by how far I have come.

First, I got into the MidJourney beta. MidJourney is an AI art generator that allows you to type a prompt and, within seconds, receive amazing art that looks as if an artist drew it. MidJourney is just one of several AI art generation apps; others include DALL-e, Stable Diffusion, and Wombo.

In experimenting with the app, I was amazed at how easy it was to use. In fact, it really is as easy as typing in what you want and getting amazing results. If you want a picture of a model wearing a leather jacket, then type that in and be prepared to be amazed. If you want a science fiction landscape in the style of a certain artist, then all you have to do is use the right keywords. This has democratized art and made it so that anyone can generate art as long as they can type. I believe this is truly a watershed moment for the Internet.

Second, I have begun working with a mentor who is quite

adept at cover design. He has offered to help me learn the tools of the trade. I promptly took him up on that offer.

Third, I invested in several cover design courses. The first course was focused on the concept of cover design. It also taught me how to think about art and some additional considerations to get quality art every time. Part of this course also taught me how to design my own covers for the first time.

I have some Photoshop experience, but I am I no means proficient at it. To rectify this, I took a book cover Photoshop course from Neo Stock. It taught me how to do some basic compositing, which is a critical design skill.

I also took a cover design course from Udemy that gave me additional context and tools to think about when designing covers.

And of course, I watched several hours' worth of YouTube videos covering different tools and techniques. These supplemented items from the courses.

Am I a professional cover designer? No, but I have a knowledge base I can leverage in 2023. This journey will consist of many steps, and I'm proud to say that I took those first critical steps this quarter.

EXPERIMENTS WITH AI-GENERATED ART

I've written in previous volumes my fascination with artificial intelligence-generated art. I discussed the program DALL-e, which represents a new wave of art creation. This quarter, I had the pleasure of experimenting with MidJourney, which is a competitor to DALL-e.

MidJourney is a program that takes your text and turns it into art. You type in what you want to see, and the AI generates a compelling image. These are called "prompts."

Examples of prompts include:

- a dog dressed as Napoleon in the style of an oil painting
- an angry crystal dragon in a shimmering quartz cave
- a cyberpunk pirate
- and more.

You can type in virtually anything. You will get amazing results if you craft the prompt correctly.

The most compelling part of MidJourney is that there is a seemingly endless number of attributes that you can apply to your art. For example, if I want to create a portrait in the style of the great artist John Singer Sargent, I can just type that in. If I don't like that and I want a portrait in the style of modern artist Chuck Close, I can just swap out the names. I can also tell the AI to generate a photorealistic portrait and even tell it what type of camera and lens to use. The choices are staggering and only limited to your imagination.

MidJourney also does textures. If I want to create a bleached oak floorboard texture, I can do that and even tell MidJourney how wide the floorboards should be.

MidJourney also paints landscapes, so if I want a rustic countryside in the style of a 90s anime, I can do that too.

As I said, the options are endless.

There is now a vibrant community of people creating art with AI art generators who have never picked up a pencil to draw in their lives (me being one of them). This is revolutionary, and I don't think people truly realize how seismic these programs are.

Millions of people worldwide have concepts in their heads but will never be able to draw or paint them. They're not artists by heart. If they're creative, they often don't have the funds to pay an artist, or, they may have difficulty finding the right artist for the vision in their head. For the artist they do hire, they have to worry about the artists meeting their deadlines, communicating effectively, and other issues that come up throughout the artistic process, such as delays.

AI-generated art has now removed those barriers. Now, anyone can come up with a concept and render it in seconds. Case in point: I taught my daughter how to use MidJourney, and within 30 minutes, we had both creative art that would have cost us tens of thousands of dollars to make if we had commissioned someone.

This is a big deal. Make no mistake—these programs are

enjoying a lot of hype right now. The hype will die down as people get bored with it or find another fad to chase, but the technology is here to stay. The art world will never be the same.

Decades from now, people will look back and draw a sharp line through history: everything before 2022 and everything after.

I think this is good, but I understand why artists are afraid and concerned about their livelihoods. AI art is perhaps the most salient example of artificial intelligence taking away someone's job.

In previous volumes, I discussed the impacts of artificial intelligence audiobooks, which has narrators understandably concerned. However, in the conversation about that medium, no one *seriously* thinks that AI audiobooks will completely displace narrators. It will affect them, sure, but there will always be a need for well-narrated audio. The technology has a long way to go before it replaces someone like Scott Brick.

I've also talked about artificial intelligence-assisted writing apps like Sudowrite. Sudowrite uses the GPT-3 model (at the time of this writing), generating short bursts of text based on a small sample of your writing. While I expect this technology to advance rapidly over the next decade, I also don't believe that anyone *seriously* believes that Sudowrite will put writers out of a job. At least right now.

I cannot confidently say that about AI art. Here's the problem: it generates art within seconds that would take an artist months to generate.

It also generates art that may also be physically impossible to create. For example, say that you want to create a piece in the style of Dadaism. This art style is based on cutting out pieces of paper and styling them. While an artist can accomplish this digitally, it would take them a lot of time. It takes an AI seconds.

Everything is just a few keystrokes away...If you want an

acrylic painting, type it in, and the AI will convert the image. If you change your mind and want a skeuomorphic style, the AI will change it. There's just no competing against the AI's speed.

There are some failings with the technology that are likely to be short term. First, there's not much control over how models and buildings look. If you type in a church, the AI will determine what the church will look like. You can assign certain descriptors to it, but you can't tailor the design much from what you see. This is also true of models and colors.

Next, you can't design images with any consistency. You can use the same keywords and prompts, but each image will look different in its own way. Therefore, you can't create a consistent gallery of images. In my mind, this is the poison pill for the technology right now. I have every suspicion that this will not be the case in a few years.

Next, the AI doesn't provide layered photo files, so what you see is what you get. At some point, I'm betting you'll be able to download Photoshop files of your art, which will take this to a completely different level.

Also, the technology isn't perfect. Sometimes it doesn't get faces right. It has a difficult time rendering fingers, for example. It also doesn't do well with feet. But these are challenges that will dissipate over time.

I feel like the *Indie Author Confidential* series so far has spotlighted different industries whose occupation is at risk due to AI advancements. That's unfortunate, but there's very little we can do about it.

As a writer, my only solace in AI art is that, for the time being, the act of being a writer is still pretty secure. Even if someone could type in a few sentences and get a novel generated in a few seconds, AI advancement is not sophisticated enough to generate text that is grammatically correct, sufficiently creative, or coherent at the moment. Right now, it reads like enlightened gibberish.

Will that change? Absolutely, but the biggest thing we have going for us is that someone can't just generate a book and then sell it. They have to read it first and make sure that it makes sense. That takes time. It's also drastically different from AI art, which can be consumed in seconds. Again, we have this going for us.

As I watch MidJourney and DALL-e evolve, I'm making a few observations about how the industry is shifting:

- The technology is democratizing art. People who were never artists can now be amazing ones.
- A community is springing up to help non-artists create effective prompts for the AI. This is called "prompt crafting." I predict that non-artists will be willing to pay money for good prompts written by artists and non-artists alike.
- Non-artists don't want to go through the trouble of learning the nuances of prompt crafting, so they will rely on other people to do it, creating a new cottage industry where you can hire someone on a site like Fiverr or Upwork and tell them what you need so they can generate the prompts for you.
- The prompts aren't perfect, so many people will hire artists to touch up and fix issues generated by the AI.
- This is transforming artistry from a creative profession into a service profession.

Those are just a few of the observations. From that, I can draw the following conclusions:

- Learning AI art and how to generate effective art with prompts will be critical. You will be able to use this art in every area of your writing business (book covers, blog articles, etc.).
- Understanding how to manipulate photos in Photoshop, Affinity Designer, or other similar software is now an essential skill for authors.
- This is the future of stock photos.
- This is the future of book covers.
- Authors will soon be hiring designers not to create their book covers, but to correct covers generated by AIs.
- Cover designers will also begin using AI technology in their designs, saving them time, effort, and money. There will be a big difference between designers who design the traditional way and designers who use AI and clean up the generations. How will you know which caliber of designer you're dealing with? Should you pay the same price for an AI designer as a traditional designer? This is going to shake up the market and create additional pricing tiers. Or, at least, it should. This is much-needed, because, as I have been saying for the last two years in this series, the price of cover design is out of control.

I have never been more excited about a technology than I have with AI art. When I first discovered it last year, I was intrigued. When I followed up on it, I was fascinated. Now that I can try for myself, I am enthralled. I highly suggest you check it out because this will be a portent for things to come.

MORE MATH BEHIND COVER DESIGN

It's time to do some more math on cover design. With the advent of AI art being a viable path now, the game has changed. As I keep saying (almost to the point of nauseum), the costs of cover designs continue to rise, and they will one day be unaffordable for the average author (one could argue that they already are). This is a shame because self-publishing is about democratizing this profession—the glory of it is that anyone, anywhere can self-publish a book with low cost and low effort compared to a traditional publisher. That glory is diminishing more every day, and the future will belong to those authors who can insulate themselves from this coming threat.

Let's do some math.

HIRING A DESIGNER

We'll use the same scenario for all the examples I'm going to give in this chapter.

We're going to assume that you publish four books per year, and each cover costs $600, representing the current average costs of three major cover designers I've been following. (If I were doing this exercise in 2018, I could have used $300 as a benchmark. That goes to show you just how expensive it is getting.)

We'll also assume a three-month wait for each cover.

So, to recap:

- 4 covers
- $600 per cover, or $2,400 per year
- Three-month waiting period
- Five hours of your time, or 300 minutes
- Total: $2,400 per year

Doing Your Own Covers

The costs to create 4 book covers are as follows:

- $600/year for the Adobe Creative Suite
- $100 for 100 stock images
- No waiting period
- 2 hours (120 minutes) to find art and design each cover, or 8 hours total (480 minutes)
- Total: $700 per year

DOING YOUR OWN COVERS WITH AI ART

This is a slight variation of the previous method.

- $600/year for the Adobe Creative Suite
- $600/year for an AI art service
- No waiting period
- 2 hours (120 minutes) to find art and design each cover, or 8 hours total (480 minutes)

- Total: $1,250 per year

COMPARING THE METHODS

The math becomes very clear when you compare the methods:

- Hiring a Designer: $2,400/year
- Doing Your Own Covers with AI Art: $1,250/year
- Doing Your Own Covers the Traditional Way: $700/year

You can argue the value of a designer all you want, but you can't argue with the math, especially if the quality of AI art is as good, if not better, than a designer.

AI art provides quality art at a fraction of the cost of a designer, and you can create as many covers as you want.

Remember, the $2,400 per year design costs will not be constant. Five years from now, it could very well be $4,800 or more. You might be able to afford cover designs now, but that may not be true in the future, even for affluent authors.

If the benchmark of an affluent author is $100,000 per year, then $2,400 in design costs per year represents 2.4 percent of their gross annual income. When you account for taxes at 25 percent, it becomes 3 percent. And that's being generous. And, again, at the risk of repeating myself, this is just for four books.

When design costs double again in a few years, the costs will account for almost 5 percent of a $100,000 gross annual income and almost 7 percent of net. Add in other business expenses and the costs of living, and you can see why this is an existential threat.

How does this compare to other professions that must also hire vendors to complete essential services? It's hard to know. I did some research, but it's difficult to make apples-to-apples comparisons. What I do know, however, is that having a vendor whose pricing is so variable is a business problem that a savvy businessperson would move to rectify so that they can minimize the impact of price increases or swings. No author I know is doing that.

As I said, this is unsustainable in just the short term.

BOOK PREVIEW APP

Authors need a better way to offer book previews on their websites. Amazon has offered an embedded preview tool for years; you install the code on your computer, and readers can preview and purchase your book directly from your sales page on Amazon. It's an elegant way to sell books.

I have been surprised over the last few years that other retailers haven't allowed similar functionality. This seems like something that Apple, Kobo, Barnes & Noble, and Google Play would have copied.

They haven't.

The only reliable way to offer book previews on your site is to use Amazon's tool, which is not ideal.

It would be great if there were a tool that functioned similarly to Amazon's but gave readers a call to action at the end to purchase the book from whatever retailer they buy their books from. A tool like this seems right up Draft2Digital's alley.

I've been looking for a tool that can accomplish this purpose, but I haven't found one yet, so I've been thinking about how to accomplish this manually. One idea is to upload a PDF with an attractive call to action at the end and then embed that PDF using an existing PDF viewer tool. That may be the only way to solve this problem until someone develops a better solution.

ADDITIONAL THOUGHTS ON SALES
TRACKING FOR AUTHORS

In 2020, I developed a way to automate my sales reports. I wrote about it in previous volumes of this series, but here is a recap.

As an indie author, I receive over a dozen sales reports from the book retailers I sell at, affiliate platforms, and other miscellaneous revenue streams such as Patreon, direct sales, and paid speaking engagements.

Before 2020, I had to manually calculate all the royalties for each of my books and put that data on a summary worksheet.

Once I put my data on a summary worksheet, I analyzed it for insights. This often took me several hours per month, and it was tedious. In fact, I often neglected it because it was so painful.

I developed a workflow that allowed me to apply Microsoft Excel macros to standardize the data in my sales reports and then feed that data into a database that I could use to run reports. The process eliminated the manual data entry, sped up the process of aggregating my reports, and made my life 100 percent easier. It is still the method I use today.

I have noticed a few changes in the author sales tracking

market that are worth noting. First, there has been an increase in the use of a service that tracks all your sales online through a browser extension. I won't mention the name of the company because this is not meant to be a critique of this specific company; rather, this is a critique of the method itself. This method of sales aggregation provides much of the automation that authors seek, and there is no doubt that it makes the process easier.

However, I am not a fan of browser extensions for a few reasons:

•You are effectively handing over your sales data to another company. Who knows what they are going to do with it?

•The company you give your data to could be hacked, no matter how much they swear they won't be. Just look at the statistics of cybersecurity attacks. No matter how ardently developers insist they won't be targets, the math is not in their favor.

•Having your sales data hacked and made publicly available could be devastating. I believe this data is best kept private.

This is why I am not on the browser extension sales tracking bandwagon. I believe developers approach this problem with good faith, but I haven't seen any evidence yet that such a service would not be vulnerable to cyber-attacks. Such an attack would create a massive headache. I do use one service's browser extension tool for sales tracking, but that is for Amazon only. The issue remains, and I choose to take that risk because it makes running profitable Amazon ads much easier, but it is still a risk that I probably won't engage in the long term.

In my book the *Author Income Problem*, I wrote that it is highly unlikely that someone will solve this problem for authors in a way that does not involve a moderate level of risk. As such, it is up to every author to learn how to solve this problem for themselves in a way that minimizes their time and allows them to glean insights into the nature of their book sales.

I'm still convinced that this is the case. I hoped that current sales tracker programs on the market would continue to improve, but that hasn't happened. I still believe that the best solution to this problem is one that resides locally on your hard drive and does not transmit data over the Internet. That's why I liked the concept of one such app on the market, but it is no longer supported, and it does not calculate sales data correctly. While not perfect, this method preserves your privacy while giving you flexibility and insights into your sales data.

But alas, it cannot be.

STREAM DECK REVISITED

Last year, I purchased an Elgato Stream Deck. It is a high-tech equivalent of a macro pad, a device with physical buttons that you press to perform functions on your computer without using your keyboard or mouse.

Let me illustrate why macro pads exist. For example, if you want to copy text, you can do it one of a few ways:

- Right-click and select copy.
- Use the keyboard shortcut Ctrl + C or CMD+ C.
- Use a menu in whichever program you are using, such as Edit<Copy.

Those options are perfectly fine, but they're not ideal because they require you to stop what you're doing and find the command or keys you need. Few people have the skill to do this by memory.

A macro pad provides a techy yet clever solution for this problem by giving you a one-button solution. In the example I used, I could map Ctrl+C or CMD+ C to one button so that the button controls the command. I can also add additional commands to the button so that it acts like a switch. I could set it up so that the first button press initiates the "select all" command, the second press initiates the "copy" command, and the third press initiates a "paste" command. It saves time and effort.

This technology has been around for a very long time, works extremely well, and solves productivity problems that many people have—assuming they're willing to purchase a new tool, go through the learning curve, and commit to using it.

I like the Stream Deck because it is dynamic. You can program the buttons to change depending on which app is in the foreground. Therefore, you can have one set of buttons for Chrome, another set for Photoshop, another set for PowerPoint, and so on.

I've used my Stream Deck almost exclusively for streaming for the last year. That has been a great use case, but I kept thinking I could do more with the technology.

This quarter, I finally figured out how to maximize my Stream Deck.

Since moving to Microsoft Word as my primary writing app this year, I have adopted many macros and keyboard shortcuts to help me be more productive. I use these tools, especially when I am writing short stories. I mapped many shortcuts and macros to buttons on my Stream Deck.

Here are some examples:

- I can now run my dictation macro with a button.
- I can get a word count for a string of selected text or an entire document.
- I can toggle the spellchecker.
- I can pull up a dictionary or Google.
- I can select all text, copy, and paste with a three-way switch.

- I can activate the Read Aloud function, helping me catch invisible typos.
- I can launch the macro window to select a macro to run. This normally would have required me to navigate to the Developer tab on the Ribbon and select the macro button, which was time-consuming if I was in the middle of a task.
- I can switch between apps on my Mac.
- I can activate Word's built-in Dictation feature.

And that's just Microsoft Word.

With conference call apps such as Zoom, I can mute and unmute my microphone, turn my camera on and off, share my screen, and more—with the press of a button.

In short, the Stream Deck turned out to be one of my best investments in 2021 that I am only fully realizing now.

But it gets better. I discovered that Elgato released a new product called the Stream Deck Pedal, which is a USB switch activated by your foot. It sits underneath your desk, and you use it like a guitarist would use a foot pedal. It has three programmable buttons, much like the Stream Deck, and the buttons are dynamic and change depending on which app is in the foreground.

I immediately purchased one because it has so many benefits.

For starters, when I use the Stream Deck, I like to have my right hand on my mouse and my left hand on my keyboard. This way, I can activate whichever button I need on the Stream Deck with my left hand. But sometimes, I don't like removing my left hand from the keyboard. The foot pedal serves that purpose.

Here are some examples of how I use it:

- When streaming, I use the foot pedal to advance my graphics and mute my mic if I cough. Muting my microphone with a foot pedal is a godsend.
- When editing in Microsoft Word, I can use the foot pedal to engage editing commands such as accepting track changes, initiating macros, and even formatting text.
- When editing videos and audio, I can use the foot pedal to help me achieve commands faster.
- When designing book covers in Photoshop, I can map commonly used commands to the foot pedal to use it in tandem with the Stream Deck.

I love technology because if you look hard enough and are willing to do things differently, you can find suitable solutions to your problems.

UPGRADING MY MICROPHONE

One of my biggest pain points with my studio configuration was my microphone. When I upgraded my studio in 2021, I felt that I had made a good decision in selecting my camera, desk, and other accessories. I did not, however, purchase the right microphone. That microphone was an Audio Technica AT2035, which is a great one in its own right, but it was not the right one for me.

The Audio Technica was a condenser mic, and condenser mics are extremely sensitive. They pick up everything. That's part of their charm because you can hear subtle nuances and instruments and singers' voices. However, for radio, podcasting, and broadcasting, they are terrible choices because you can hear everything. This microphone picked up everything in my background: my furnace, laptop fan, and even my next-door neighbor's thoughts.

After thorough research, I picked up a Shure SM7B dynamic microphone, which is a much better fit for my situation.

Boy, did it make a big difference. It captures my voice while ignoring most of my background. It also makes my voice sound fuller and more robust.

However, I needed to take an additional step to improve my audio quality further. I hired an audio engineer to listen to samples of my voice recorded with the new microphone and apply noise reduction, equalization, de-essing, and compression to my voice so that it sounded radio-quality. The engineer provided preset files that I could then plug into my existing applications to sweeten my voice live.

I picked up a pair of applications called Audio Hijack and Loopback that "hijack" the microphone audio at the source, apply the effects to sweeten the signal, and then reroute the sound to the application of my choice, be it Zoom, GoToMeeting, or eCamm Live. The apps work amazingly well, and the engineer did a great job. I am so much happier with my audio now, and I feel like I have leveled up in this area.

Ironically, even with my old condenser microphone, I frequently received compliments from people about the high quality of my audio, but I knew I could do better. Now, I feel like I have turned over all the stones. Because I want to eventually return to YouTube on a semi-regular schedule in 2023, this will be an important step toward doing that. I also have plans to do more online courses and speaking engagements, so this microphone is an investment that will pay for itself.

Out of all the things I have purchased in my writing career, I have never had to worry about microphones. When I purchased my first microphone—a Blue Yeti—I was worried about whether it would be worth spending the $120 required. I was wrong. The Blue Yeti blew the rinky-dinky headset I was using out of the water, giving me amazing-sounding audio overnight. Even the Audio Technica microphone paid for itself because it allowed me to record my first audiobook, which has

since recouped the investment. I am positive that this Shure
SM7B will do the same, if not more.

WHISPER: A WATERSHED MOMENT IN AI TRANSCRIPTION

A friend recommended that I check out Whisper narration, a new service released by OpenAI in Q3 2022. He said that I would be pleasantly surprised.

The link he sent me was a playground that promised to accurately transcribe any YouTube video; all I had to do was insert a link. I found a random, educational video with voiceover narration; I inserted the link into the tool, and waited about two minutes.

The result almost made me spit out my tea. It was astounding, and I don't use that word lightly.

The narration was not only accurate, but it was punctuated. All the commas and periods were in exactly the right places. To say it was grammatically correct was an understatement. While there were a few errors here and there, it looked virtually no different from if I had sat at my computer and typed exactly what the narrator said.

It appears that AI has reached yet another watershed moment that will have implications for authors, though most won't realize it for some time.

It's no secret that I use dictation skillfully to write my books.

Fortunately, my computer is powerful enough to run Parallels, which is a virtual machine application that allows me to run Windows on my computer side-by-side next to Mac applications. Because of this, I have Dragon Professional Individual, the preeminent dictation software that, at the time of this writing, is only available on Windows operating systems. So, I get the best of both worlds.

However, many of my Mac friends aren't so lucky. Nuance Software used to make a version of Dragon for Macs, but it was always an inferior version, and it has been discontinued with no plans to revive it soon. When you also consider that Microsoft now owns Nuance Software (acquired in 2021), then you can see why the situation is especially dire for Mac users. Dragon has a mobile version called Dragon Anywhere, but it has significant downsides and is not as accurate.

So, the result has been that Mac users have not had a real dictation solution since Dragon for Mac was discontinued. Sure, there are services like Google Voice Typing, but it's not Dragon. Not by a long shot.

Also, while dictation features on phones have improved significantly in recent years, they also don't offer the functionality that Dragon does. If you're lucky enough to own a Google Pixel phone, that phone does have a transcription feature that I have heard rivals Dragon, but Google Pixel phones only represent a small market share. And if you're a Mac user, you may not own a Google phone or even want one.

That brings us back to OpenAI's Whisper narration model. Like all AI applications, it can be integrated into other applications using the Python programming language.

This means that:

1. Future uses of AI applications will not depend on operating systems because Python is universal (at least as I understand it).
2. A developer could, in theory, *very easily* develop a simple application that allows you to upload dictated audio files locally on your machine and get amazing transcription results in the same amount of time that it would take Dragon to transcribe audio (if not faster).
3. All of this can be accomplished *today*, with very little programming knowledge and expertise.

I could hire a programmer on a site like Upwork tomorrow and pay them to develop an application that utilizes the Whisper API to create a Mac application that followed the following steps:

1. Get dictated audio from a specified folder or allow the user to select a file or batch of files.
2. Run those files through the Whisper API.
3. Display the output in a text file and save that file in the same directory as the audio (or a directory of the user's choosing).

And that's it. Now, the user doesn't need Dragon at all. Oh, and did I mention that the Whisper API is free (for now)? I have some concerns about that, to be sure, but I also think that Mac authors can take advantage of this leap forward in technology to finally achieve dictation if they have previously been unable to do so.

There is another very good reason for migrating to the Whisper platform. As I mentioned previously, Microsoft has acquired Nuance Software, and the fate of Dragon is in question. Microsoft has introduced a dictation feature into its Office suite. I've tested it, and it is pretty good. Not quite as good as Dragon, but still very good. You don't have to do too many mental gymnastics to predict that Microsoft will eventually retire Dragon and integrate it into Microsoft Office. If that happens, Mac users are especially screwed. Or maybe not, but knowing the rivalry between Microsoft and Apple, they're probably screwed. Windows has always had the superior versions of Microsoft Office applications, and I don't see that changing anytime soon.

The worst part about the Microsoft Office suite at this time is that it doesn't offer transcription. There is a podcast/interview transcription feature, but it inserts awkward timestamps into your text. One day, Microsoft will probably get smart and integrate Dragon's transcription technology into its dictation suite. When that happens, goodbye Dragon.

The end of Dragon may not be so bad; after all, most authors are already using Microsoft Word in some capacity anyway, even if they use a dedicated writing app like Scrivener. However, there is a doomsday scenario in which Dragon is no longer available, and users cannot access the same level of dictation and transcription quality that they're used to.

Whisper solves this problem. I think it is a smart strategy for me to develop an operating system-agnostic method of transcription that will allow me to avoid becoming a victim of Microsoft's whims. It's just a good business strategy. I refuse to be one of those authors who gets hit with a sledgehammer and can no longer continue my preferred way of working. Not gonna happen.

Therefore, I have committed to developing a personal Mac-based application powered by Whisper to give myself options. Also, I consider moving to Whisper a technological enhancement because of the punctuation. It's possible in the future that

I may not need to speak Dragonese. If that happens, then the speed of my dictation will improve by somewhere between 20 and 30 percent, and so will the accuracy of my transcription. Imagine never having to speak a comma or period again and rarely having to fix them. That's incredible.

There is another, less visible watershed moment here that I think will also positively impact authors. One of the biggest problems with Natural Language Processing (NLP) is that it struggles with the grammatical structure of English. I wrote in previous volumes that it would be nice if I could develop an application that could police commas and punctuation. Sadly, the technology cannot do that. If it could, Microsoft Word's Editor and Grammarly would do a much better job of ensuring users adhere to proper comma usage. In my mind, there's no good reason why Grammarly still confuses the words "to" and "too."

I don't know how the team at OpenAI did it, but they seem to have figured out this punctuation and grammatical structure problem. After all, all the commas are in the right places and used correctly!

Whatever they did, I see this potentially coming to apps like Grammarly in the future. In fact, I potentially see Grammarly becoming a legacy app. We will look back on the days when we thought tools like Grammarly and ProWritingAid were state-of-the-art. What's coming is going to make them look like child's play.

If you think about it, we have artificial intelligence writing apps that recommend grammatically correct, sometimes useful text that is getting more useful every day. We also have artificial intelligence transcription. What we don't *truly* have yet is artificial intelligence editing. Grammarly is the best we have right now; frankly, while it's good, it could be much better.

The day that an artificial intelligence editor arrives, that will be a game changer. If it comes through an API, that will be even better.

I don't believe that this technology can or should replace a human editor. But a human editor's time is best spent fixing things that a computer can't detect, like advanced grammar and story issues. I believe advancements in AI editing will allow editors to work faster and focus on the things that really matter —not policing Oxford commas and comma splices.

I am very excited about the future of AI transcription. I believe this is a watershed moment, and I think more watershed moments will come.

THE POWER OF DIGITAL
HIGHLIGHTERS

I like to joke that I went to college at the wrong time and that I also went to college at the right time.

I went to college at the right time because the Internet was not as prominent in the lives of college students as it is today. While I had a laptop computer and used digital applications extensively to write papers and take care of my everyday college responsibilities, life between 2006 and 2010 was still very manual. E-books as we know them didn't exist; if you wanted a book, you had to go to the library. And in those days, the library still had the Dewey Decimal system. You couldn't look things up like you can today, so you had to find the book you were looking for and actually page through it to figure out what was relevant.

I am old enough to remember when you had to do citations manually, and professors policed your Works Cited page to ensure you got them right. Now, I'm 100 percent positive that a college student can use a program to generate their Works Cited page before turning it in to a professor.

I like to think that going to college when I did benefited me because I still have an appreciation and affection for the print medium. Though I don't read paperback books often anymore, I understand them and understand people who prefer them. I also understand the reluctance to give up the tactile sensation that paper provides.

My college years were also a time before smartphones. The iPhone wasn't introduced until I was a junior in college. In those days, if you wanted to do something with someone, you had to *do something with someone*. You had to call them on the phone. If you wanted to plan your day, you had to plan your day with a detective pad, your brain, or a physical planner. Sure, kids use planners today, but they have so many more options.

I also like to think that I went to college at the wrong time because I have such an affinity for technology that I would have been dangerous as a college student with some of the tools that are out there today.

Exhibit number one: digital notebooks like Evernote, Microsoft OneNote, and Bear. I was an early adopter of Evernote when it hit the market around 2010. Unfortunately, I had already graduated from college, but if I had been in college, I would have used the hell out of Evernote. It would have made everything so much easier. I could have had notebooks for each of my classes, used the Evernote Web Clipper to do research for projects and essays, and so much more. It could have been my college yearbook that, because Evernote is still around today, would still be accessible for me to review all these years later. That's a beautiful thing.

Exhibit number two: digital smart pens. The LiveScribe pen came out also in 2010, right around the time I graduated. It was a smart pen that used special paper to turn everything you wrote into a digital counterpart. It also had a microphone on it so that you could record your lectures while taking notes. Even cooler, you could tap a section of your notes and play back the audio that was recorded while you were writing that note.

Seriously, smart pens were such cool technology, and it's a shame that they didn't take off more than they did. As a college student, I probably would have owned several of them.

Exhibit number three: Rocketbooks. These are a variation on smart pens. They are smart notebooks requiring special gel pens that serve the same purpose. You can turn anything you write into a digital note for better safekeeping.

Trust me that there are many other technologies that I would have used in college to become the best version of myself. But the technology I want to talk about now is one that would have truly been a game changer: digital highlighters.

A digital highlighter is a handheld device with a scanner that you can use to scan text directly into a computer within seconds. Imagine reading a book, highlighting a section, and the text you highlighted popping up on your computer seconds later, with the ability to listen to it as well. You could highlight text directly into Microsoft Word or Evernote. This would've saved me so much time.

A digital highlighter solves one of the problems I have had recently: studying mega bestsellers effectively.

While traveling, I stumbled upon a reading library in a hotel with several novels from authors that I love. At the time, I was studying openings, and I was interested in reviewing at least 100 openings from mega bestsellers to see how I could improve my skill in this area. A digital highlighter would have been amazing to have because I could have taken a book off the shelf, scanned the first two or three pages directly into my phone, and had that text available to review later.

If I want to do something like that today without a digital highlighter, I have to sit down in front of my computer and type the opening of the book. Or, I have to take a picture of the first few pages, run those pictures through an OCR application to turn the image into text (which is not always accurate), or—and this is a bridge too far that I would not cross—I would have to find an EPUB version of the book, find a way to get it onto my device, and then copy the text that way. When you consider that DRM protects most traditionally published books, that means I would have to break the DRM. I'm no fan of DRM, and I don't use it in my books, but I don't believe in circumventing the technology. Plus, it's a violation of book retailers' terms of service.

So, there is no easy way to study the works of other authors at this point without some effort. A digital highlighter can help solve that problem. At the time of this writing, they are pricey at $149, but I think the investment could be worth it one day just for the time you would save. Imagine going to the library, picking a random book off the shelf from a mega bestseller, scanning a random two or three pages, and then taking it home to analyze potential techniques. Of course, I believe you should read a book before studying it, but sometimes you don't need to.

I like digital highlighters a lot, and I will probably purchase one in the future.

THE CASE FOR A WRITING COMPUTER NOT CONNECTED TO THE INTERNET

I have heard many successful writers advocate for a writing computer that is not connected to the Internet. Jonathan Franzen recommended this in a magazine article interview once, and it struck me as a bit eccentric, and I rejected the idea outright at the time.

Prolific author Dean Wesley Smith has also recommended writing on a computer that is not connected to the Internet. His rationale is that it is a useful trick to get into the "writing" mindset quickly. After all, if you have a dedicated writing computer, you will also have a dedicated writing desk, which means that when you sit down at the desk and fire up that computer, you will be ready to write because you will condition your brain over time to transition into creative mode. When Jonathan Franzen said it, I was young and naive and didn't understand why anyone would do this, but when I heard Dean say it, I was a working writer and understood the wisdom behind it.

During a YouTube video interview with Stephen King, I also heard John Grisham express a similar concern about having a dedicated writing computer. Grisham's rationale was completely different: he recommended it for security purposes. Since he is one of the best-selling authors in the world, he is terrified of someone hacking his computer and stealing his manuscripts and other valuable data. That to me is perhaps the best reason to have a dedicated writing computer not connected to the Internet, but then again, we are all not John Grisham.

Cybersecurity attacks against businesses are on the rise, though. I've said this for a while: the data clearly shows that small businesses are the biggest targets for cybersecurity attacks such as hacking, malware, and ransom attacks. This is because small businesses do not have the resources or technical expertise to protect their networks. It is out of sight and out of mind because small business owners have a million other things to do.

I've also said this for a while: authors are small businesses. It's just a matter of time before the self-publishing sector gets hit with a string of cybersecurity attacks that will destroy everyone's innocence and naivety. We are currently living in a golden era, the equivalent of living in a small town and being able to leave your door unlocked at night without any fear of getting burglarized. I would dare say that the technical times we live in as authors are Edenic. It won't be this way forever, and it pays to start investing in your cybersecurity today. I even dedicated an entire online course that is criminally under-viewed called "Writing in Hard Times" which attempts to help authors think about this vulnerability so they can take the meaningful first steps in protecting their data, platforms, and readers. However, this is still out of sight and out of mind for most authors because they don't think something like this could ever happen to them. In fact, I bet the thought hasn't even crossed many people's minds. But the threat is very real.

Back to Grisham. I think John Grisham has the best rationale for maintaining a writing computer that exists in a vacuum. I don't know for sure how John Grisham operates, but here is my best guess:

- John writes his novels and new material on this dedicated computer. He never connects it to the Internet, and if I were a betting man, I would guess that he has had the network card physically removed so that connecting to the Internet is not even possible. As his computer ages, he just purchases a new one.
- When he finishes a manuscript, he downloads it onto a password-protected USB thumb drive—make that two thumb drives. He then ships the drive from a non-obvious address to his publisher in New York via certified mail, with insurance. He requires a signature before the package can be delivered.
- He keeps a copy on a separate thumb drive for himself; he probably maintains a separate database and/or network of hard drives containing *all* of his work. These hard drives have never been connected to the Internet, are password-protected, and are set up in a way that only he and his heirs understand. If he is as paranoid as I think he is, he probably has his manuscripts both at his home and at another off-site location just in case anything were to happen.
- When his publisher receives the manuscript, they either have very lax controls or follow strict protocols themselves (I would bet on the former). If it's the former, then his editors also work on computers not connected to the Internet. The only time the manuscript comes online is when it is

formatted and ready for the printer, which is often many months before the publication date, but this creates a tight seal so that the manuscript does not leak. But I'm just speculating on how the publisher operates.

- Rinse and repeat.

Of course, I'm just playing a guessing game here. I don't know about Grisham's security protocols, but if I were him, those would be the protocols I would follow.

So, have I come around to a dedicated writing computer? Not quite.

For a tech-savvy author like me, the concept is brilliant in theory but poses several practical problems.

First, I am not John Grisham. While I am certainly a target for attacks just like anyone else, I doubt anyone will go out of their way to make that happen. Therefore, the need for a dedicated writing computer is minimal because the risk is minimal. If I won a prestigious award or started selling at a higher level, then the calculus would change.

Also, it's just inconvenient. It means you have to have two computers and two writing desks. That's no good. I have space but would rather not clutter it with multiple desks.

The logistics also pose a challenge, given that I work with all of my editors and freelancers online. Unless my editor was willing to operate within the constraints that I outlined above, it would be impractical, increase my editing costs, and also drastically increase the production times for my books. There would be no way to have complete privacy over the book. As much as we like to think there is such a thing as privacy in today's digital age, it is a mere illusion.

So, this isn't practical for me at this time, but it's something I reserve the right to think about more deeply in the future as my career and needs change. It's also something I recommend other authors consider as well.

That said, I do like the wisdom of Dean Wesley Smith's advice, and I do believe it would be a useful trick if one could figure out the logistic problems I discussed in this chapter.

HOTEL LIBRARIES AND LITTLE FREE LIBRARIES

While traveling this quarter, I stumbled upon a reading library in a hotel. It was a massive bookcase filled with hardcovers by all the big-name authors. There was a mix of thrillers, suspense, and romance.

I kicked myself that I forgot to bring one of my books. If I had, I would have left it in the reading library. I have been meaning to do this, but I always forget to grab a few of my paperback books before I walk out the door to hit the road.

You never know who is going to be interested in reading your book. Assuming that you have a professional cover, book description on the back cover, and thorough editing, I see no reason why your book can't sit on the same shelf as James Patterson or Clive Cussler. The reading library I stumbled upon had a shortage of science fiction and fantasy, and it would have been a great opportunity for me to diversify that shelf!

But alas, maybe one of these days, I will get this right.

Another thing I noticed about reading libraries is that it is probably best to leave a hardcover on these types of bookshelves. I should travel with a few paperbacks and hardbacks, just in case. If most of the books on the shelves are hardcovers, then I will leave a hardcover. If most books are paperbacks, then I will leave a paperback. I think it's important to blend in. When in Rome...

I have also learned to appreciate the power of Little Free Libraries. These are libraries that people can construct and put in their front yards. Pedestrians and passersby can look at the library, take a book, and leave a book. They are a wonderful thing, and I have seen a proliferation of these Little Free Libraries in my city of Des Moines, Iowa. Again, as I write this chapter, I am kicking myself because I still have not taken advantage of this opportunity. It would cost me very little to, for example, print 50 authors copies of my books, spend an afternoon driving around, and inserting them in every Little Free Library that I can find. Sure, I have to pay for author's copies and shipping, but what do I have to lose?

In my upcoming book on marketing, I dedicated an entire chapter to hotel libraries and Little Free Libraries. I will post it here.

———

I don't know if this is true everywhere, but over the last decade, I have seen a proliferation of Little Free Libraries, which are simple wooden shelves that people build in their front yards that house books. Passersby can see what's in the library, take a book, and even leave a book.

In my neighborhood, Little Free Libraries are on every corner. You can bet that I leave my books in these libraries. Why not?

While writing this chapter, I did a quick web search and discovered 25 Little Free Libraries in my zip code alone.

Another free library you should consider is the library at your local hotel or coffee shop. They frequently have shelves where you can grab free books and leave them. Leave a copy of your book on the shelf before you check out from the hotel. Even better, autograph it!

But, you really, really, *really* need to make sure that you have a great cover that looks professional and would fit in with other books in your genre. Otherwise, no one will touch your book, and the staff will probably throw it out.

You can also find these free libraries in your local coffee shops and other small business establishments, so don't disregard them.

LOOKING FORWARD

DEALING WITH A PRODUCTIVITY SLUMP

I experienced my first productivity downturn with my million-word challenge.

I wrote about this in a previous chapter where I discussed the importance of writing a short story while the idea is hot. But that was only part of the story.

My wife traveled out of town, and I was on double-parent duty for a week. My daughter had many activities going on, and I truly had to take a week off writing. I thought maybe I could achieve 25 percent or 50 percent of my quota, but that didn't happen. That in and of itself wasn't a big deal because I could still consume content and progress in other areas of my writing business. For example, I got a lot of reading done and cleared my inbox down to zero. I also fixed some issues with one of my book's sales pages. So the week wasn't a complete loss.

However, I found it extremely difficult to ramp back up to 2,750 words per day. In fact, it took another week and a half before I returned to my previous productivity levels. And even then, my word counts were often right at my quota.

I found myself frequently asking why this was. I also found, strangely, that the drive to write fiction just wasn't there.

I've been doing this long enough to know how to handle it. I would have been anxious about returning to the writing desk early in my career. I would have been anxious at the fact that I was missing my daily word count and potentially falling behind on the challenge, especially when I had worked so hard to build a surplus.

However, experience has taught me a few things. First, there are three root causes of writer's block:

1. anxiety/fear
2. lack of inspiration/boredom
3. personal circumstances

At the same time, I had water in my basement due to a leak from an old water softener unit. The leak was significant enough that it caused mold, and I had to file a claim to have part of my drywall ripped out and replaced. That was also causing some unconscious stress.

And finally, two immediate family members had health scares during that week.

So, in short, the stress of double-parent duty, homeowner woes, and family issues really put a damper on my productivity. My creative voice seized up, and it took a week and a half before it determined that it was safe to write again. It also didn't help that I wrote a story that I got stuck in the middle of—all these things culminated in a perfect storm.

Once I finished the story and got used to writing at pulp speed again, I was back into my regular routine, no problem. But it took a while.

This experience taught me the importance of building surpluses whenever I can. My rule of ABC—always be adding surplus—saved me from falling behind on the challenge. Even with a loss of writing days, I was still ahead for the year. The productivity downturn brought me close to zero, and now I must begin the process anew of building a surplus so that I can be prepared for the next time this happens.

As a writer, I go through seasons of abundance, seasons of winter, and seasons where things are pretty steady. The trick is understanding where I am and how to address each season.

If I'm in a season of abundance, I bank as many extra words as possible and prepare for winter.

If I'm in a season of winter, then I do the best I can, wait it out, and hope for the best.

If I'm in a season of steadiness, I just keep going.

That's the life of a writer. You just have to keep going.

DEALING WITH ECONOMIC DOWNTURNS

I've heard a lot of talk from writers terrified about their careers. It started during my travels to writing conferences this year. I spoke with one writer who told me that her Facebook ads were no longer working, and her income had dropped by over 50 percent. She made a living from her writing and didn't know how she would continue. This author was attending the conference in hopes of finding a new set of strategies that she could use to improve her income.

At another conference, someone mentioned offhand that authors were seeing their sales drop. I noted it, but because it wasn't true for me at the time, I didn't pay much attention to it.

Then, I heard more prominent authors lament the drop in sales. Kristine Kathryn Rusch even wrote a blog post about it, and the popular Six-Figure Authors Podcast came out of a hiatus to address the issue. Then I started really paying attention.

First, I got the data about my sales. My sales numbers are slightly up this year, but certain segments are down. It's no different from any prior years. The sad reality about being an author is that some years you're up, and some years you're down. There often isn't a rhyme or reason to it, but there are clues.

At the time of this writing, we are in a unique and challenging profit environment. The war in Ukraine is driving instability and inflation. Greedy corporations are also taking advantage of the pandemic and unfairly raising their profit, contributing to inflation.

And, of course, we have—wait for it—record inflation, which means that people have to pay more for everything, including food, fuel, energy, and rent. All readers are faced with pricing pressures in almost every area of their lives, so it's no surprise that they're spending more money on essential services and less on entertainment.

Also, in the United States, this is a midterm election year, possibly the most covered midterm in recent memory. Usually, people don't pay much attention to midterm elections. This year, almost everyone paid attention. When people are focused on politics, they aren't reading books.

So, when I thought about it, it wasn't surprising that book sales are down across the board for many authors. What was clear to me (and not clear to many of the authors lamenting this) was that sales will be back up. They always come back up. That's just the cyclical nature of the book business. The best thing that we can do is make smart long-term choices, wait out the economic "winters," and take advantage of the good times when they come.

If the book business weren't cyclical, then most authors wouldn't have careers. As long as authors continue to publish books, find readers, and do the right things even when times are hard, I don't doubt that most will continue to have careers.

This is why I have focused so much on cutting my costs, investing in automation and technology, and diversifying my income so that I am less susceptible to economic swings. I can definitely say that my strategy so far has been successful. If it weren't, I would be one of those people complaining about my sales dropping.

Here are some of the techniques I have used to insulate myself and protect my business from the ravages of inflation:

- **Don't overpay for services**. While I am a big fan of paying the right people to do a job, I don't overpay. This is critical in an unregulated market where anyone can charge whatever they want for a service.

- **Learn how to do your own book covers**. You probably knew I was going to say that, but investing the time to learn cover design will cut your costs by at least 50 percent, therefore improving your profit. This is especially helpful if the book production process is expensive for you and your sales do not completely pay for the production costs of your books.

- **Consider raising your prices, but do understand what inflation is**. Inflation is when everyone raises their prices and wages at the same time. Therefore, if you increase the price of your books, you're only contributing to the problem! That said, I understand why some authors would be tempted to do this, but in today's current environment, you can only raise the prices of your books so high. Besides, this industry is one of the few bastions where readers are complaining about increased book prices. We as authors can take advantage of that by keeping our books priced the way they are until the current inflation environment subsides.

- **Diversify, diversify, diversify**. If you're all-in with Kindle Unlimited, now's the time to start planning your escape strategy. Establishing a plan to diversify is still a smart strategy even if revenue streams do not immediately pay off. For example, if you don't have direct sales set up on your website, now is a good time to do that.
- **Cut your costs**. If you don't need it, cut it. Operate on the leanest budget that you can and carry it into the good times with you. This will ensure that you will protect your profit even if your sales decrease.

Economic downturns are not easy, but they are not forever. We will all get through this, just as we got through the last ones. The trick is to be proactive and be patient.

DESIGNING NEW BUSINESS CARDS

I found myself at a writing conference without business cards. You would think I would know better, but alas.

It has been a few years since I ordered business cards. A few things have changed. First, they have gotten more expensive, but we won't talk about that.

I ordered middle-of-the-road business cards—not the cheap ones, but not the most expensive ones either. I wanted something that presented nicely and didn't go over the top.

I settled on VistaPrint, which had the best card design experience. I didn't want to hire someone to design my cards because I will be doing a rebrand in the next few years anyway, and I will have new business cards designed at that time. I just needed something to last me for a few years. VistaPrint served that purpose at an affordable cost.

My very first business cards were poor at best. They had my name, phone number, email address, and website, but the print was too tiny, and the cards themselves were so small that they weren't effective. This time, I went with a colorful but simple design, and I opted for a QR code business card instead. This type of business card has a QR code that goes wherever you want—your website, a social media profile—you name it.

Psychologically, I like the idea of a QR business code because it is a subliminal pull. With a regular business card, the person you give it to has to remember you well enough and care about your conversation enough to go to their computer or phone and visit your website. It sounds simple enough, but it's actually a big ask. Think about all the people you meet throughout a conference. You must capitalize on someone's memory pretty thoroughly for them to follow up with you after meeting them. That rarely happens.

A QR code business card solves this problem because it reduces friction. Almost everyone is within two feet of their phone at all times, and if you use compelling copy next to your QR code, you're going to intrigue them enough to take action. And if you can get them to do that, you can increase your community, connections, and income.

So, that's why I went with a QR code business card.

I also include my face on business cards. I do this because most people will not remember faces after conferences either. When you put your face front and center on the business card, they have no choice but to remember your face. Combined with a QR code, you have an effective lead machine.

Now that I have ordered business cards like a proper author and businessperson, I have plenty to hand out and tuck in the back of my books.

THE RETURN TO MICROSOFT WORD

I wrote in a previous volume about my return to Microsoft Word as my primary writing tool. It gives me no pleasure, but Word is the best writing app to accommodate my dictation needs.

Here is my current workflow and how I am using Word to achieve my goal of writing one million words in a year.

As I have written previously, I dictate my words into a voice recorder and connect the recorder to my computer, using Dragon's Auto Transcribe Folder Agent to transcribe my voice into text. After transcription, I load the words into Microsoft Word and run my proprietary dictation macro, which cleans up the text and does the majority of the editing for me so that I only have to focus on a few stray errors. I then use Microsoft Editor, Grammarly Premium, ProWritingAid, and PerfectIt to clean up the text.

Next, I use Word's Read Aloud feature to listen to the dictated text at about 1.5 speed. When I listen to dictated text, I find common issues like dropped articles and missing words a lot easier and faster. I did some timing tests, and it took me approximately five minutes to review 500 words. Therefore,

Read Aloud keeps me on a guided track and gives me a realistic expectation of how long it will take to edit my stories.

When I have finished the story, I rerun Editor, Grammarly, ProWritingAid, and PerfectIt for good measure. Then, I observe Heinlein's Rules and ship the story off to my editor.

Microsoft Word is the best tool to help me achieve my current goals. I never thought I would be here, but sometimes fate has a way of being funny.

No other writing app on the market offers the tools I mentioned. Therefore, I will use Microsoft Word as my primary writing app for the foreseeable future. At the end of the day, all I care about is quality and quantity. I am not above using any tool that will help me achieve my goals. This is why I invest so much time in technology to be nimble.

TRAVELING TO SAUDI ARABIA

This quarter, I received a once-in-a-lifetime opportunity to travel to Saudi Arabia. I was invited to speak at the Jeddah International Book Fair, one of the largest publishing conferences in the region, with over 70,000 attendees and over 400 publishers. The theme for the event was science fiction and fantasy, and the organizers placed special emphasis on self-publishing, which is picking up steam in the Middle East.

At first, I wasn't sure if the invitation was legit. It was.

You don't hear much about Saudi Arabia. It only recently opened to foreigners. Whatever you do hear about the country on the news is not pleasant. Ultimately, I'm not here to talk about politics. I just want to help writers, wherever they are in the world.

I accepted the invitation and found myself on a frenetic pace to prepare for overseas travel. After all, I had never been to the Middle East or North Africa before, so I had to get a battery of vaccines. I also had to buy some new luggage and travel supplies. Most importantly, I had to research Middle Eastern customs, taboos, and things to watch out for while traveling. I was to be a guest in Saudi Arabia, so I fully intended to abide by the country's laws. After intense preparation and self-education about Saudi Arabia and Islam, the day finally came to step on the plane and leave the United States for the first time since the pandemic.

Twenty-three hours later, I landed in Jeddah with no contacts other than the person who was supposed to pick me up. I truly threw myself into the experience.

Despite Arabic being the official language of Saudi Arabia, almost all the signs are in English. Many people in the airports, hotels, and restaurants speak good English. The customs agent noticed that my birthplace was in Missouri. He asked me where, and I told him St. Louis. Turns out he spent four years in Illinois in college and visited St. Louis a lot when he lived in the United States. Crazy coincidence. He handed me my passport and told me to enjoy my time in Saudi Arabia.

When I arrived, the first thing I immediately noticed was all the men walking around in white thobes and the women walking around in black abayas. Some women had their faces covered, and you could see only their eyes. By my clothes alone, I was easily pegged as a foreigner.

Getting around wasn't hard. The conference sent me a shuttle from the airport to the hotel. Uber also works well in Saudi Arabia, and many of the location names are in English, so they're easy to find on the app.

I stayed at the Crowne Plaza Jeddah Al Salaam, a newer hotel in the northern part of Jeddah. It was like any modern hotel, but a little more advanced. One thing I noticed was that there were employees everywhere. You never see bellhops anymore in American hotels unless they're upscale. Here, there were at least three in the lobby. Several employees in the gym made sure the equipment was clean and the floor was dry.

Staying at this hotel was like staying at a hotel decades ago in the states. The service was excellent.

The hotel also provided complimentary meals for the speakers. The restaurant was quite large, and had beautiful white and blue Islamic tiles on the floor, with buffet-style options. There were at least ten different stations of food, serving everything from fruit, pastries, hot food from all over the world, western food like hamburgers and hot dogs, and soups and salads. The waiters served soda in bottles. Large flatscreen televisions played the World Cup games, which was happening in Qatar while I was traveling.

I met several other speakers from the United States, Canada, and Jamaica, and we stuck together. I didn't know any of the speakers previously, but I had done my homework, looking them up and watching YouTube video interviews they had done. I brushed up on my knowledge of their areas of expertise, which made for easy conversations.

A curious detail about the trip that I anticipated but took the other speakers off-guard was Arab hospitality, that was also matched by what could best be described as "hands-off." The organizers did an amazing job getting us to our destination and helping us be comfortable, but beyond that, they did nothing else. Therefore, it was up to the speakers to determine how they wanted to spend their time in the country. This was frustrating to some.

As for me, I expected it, so I made an itinerary once it was clear that there wouldn't be any planned events for the speakers other than the conference.

Places I visited included:

- the "corniches," beachfront trails along the Red Sea that locals love to visit
- the Red Sea Mall, a megamall with every shop and brand you can think of

- Al Balad, or the old city where the buildings are made of coral and sand
- The Tomb of Eve (yes, *that* Eve)
- Al Baik, a fast food franchise that sells fried chicken seasoned with saffron and turmeric
- Al Tayebat, a giant museum that could best be described as "the Smithsonian of Saudi Arabia."
- And more!

I made the most of my time and had a blast, even though I didn't speak the language. I had learned a few Arabic phrases, and those worked wonders. Simple things like "hello" and "thank you" go a long way.

I found the people to be extremely warm, hospitable, and friendly. Foreigners still aren't amazingly common, so many were curious. Many people went out of their way to say hello and to ask where I was from. They also went out of their way to help. The hospitality reminded me of the friendliness I had received in Costa Rica and Nicaragua. It's a type of kindness that you don't generally see in the United States.

And then there was the main event itself: the Digital Publishing Conference. The entire program was in Arabic, but the event provided headsets that let you listen to a real-time translator. That translator was one hard-working guy, let me tell you. Whenever someone spoke Arabic, all the English speakers put their headsets on as the translator spoke English. Whenever someone spoke in English, all the English speakers put their headsets down, and the Arabic speakers put their headsets on as the translator switched immediately to translating into Arabic. It was truly a sight to behold.

I also had to wear the headset on stage. I sat on a panel with four people who all spoke excellent English, but they spoke in Arabic for the panel since most people in the audience didn't speak English. On the panel, we talked about self-publishing in the Middle East and North Africa, and I learned a great deal about how distribution is handled in the region, what tools authors have available to them, and the process they follow to publish. It was an eye-opening hour for me.

In many ways, publishing in the Middle East reminds me of how things were in the west ten years ago. Self-publishing was accepted but not encouraged. Most people still chased the glory of traditional publishing. Yet, the authors who chose to self-publish were winning in a big way, especially those who focused on acting like traditional publishers and producing books with excellent covers, good writing, and editing, and good packaging such as book descriptions and prices.

Anecdotally, I heard from a few people that there are self-published authors in Saudi Arabia who are wiping the floor with traditional publishers, and that made me smile. Unfortunately, I didn't get to meet any of those authors. I would have paid money to talk to them.

The event organizers did a great job, and I enjoyed myself at the conference. Suddenly, it was time to go home.

My return flight was through Dallas, and (wait for it) I got stuck there. Unfortunately, a tornado near the Dallas-Fort Worth airport wreaked havoc on travel. I had to spend the night in a nearby suburb.

When I finally returned home, I felt as if I had woken up from a fever dream. I traveled to the Middle East, got to experience a part of the world that very few people have seen until this point, and immersed myself in a culture that I enjoyed. Sometimes I still don't believe I traveled there.

I'm grateful for the experience and will never forget it.

KICKSTARTER LESSONS

This year, I was part of a successful Kickstarter that funded in 36 hours. It was a short story anthology.

Kickstarter has been on my list of marketing tactics to explore for quite some time, but I haven't yet had the opportunity to get around to it. I paid careful attention to how the organizer structured the campaign, and I am recording some of the lessons I learned that I could apply to my Kickstarter campaigns when I am ready to start running them for my books.

- The organizers started planning well in advance-- around eight months.
- They communicated early and often about their marketing plans and sought ideas from the contributors.
- All the stories were finished and edited before they even considered sending the Kickstarter campaign live.
- They went into the campaign with a solid list of potential stretch goals, just in case.

- They leveraged the network of all the authors contributing to the anthology. Each author shared the campaign with their respective audiences immediately when the campaign went live. Momentum is everything with Kickstarters.
- They studied other successful campaigns to figure out what was working.
- They were thoughtful about everything throughout the process.
- They made a funny, catchy introductory video. Most Kickstarter campaigns do not fund without one.
- They delivered the goals on time and within budget.

While the Kickstarter did not raise much money, it raised a ton of money compared to the original goal. It was an astonishing success that taught me a lot about navigating this emerging platform.

AUDIO COMMENTARY REVISITED

I wrote about audio commentary in a previous volume of this series. In short, I used to love audio commentary features on DVDs, and it is malpractice that streaming sites like Netflix and Hulu have not re-adapted it for the streaming era. Commentary represents millions of hours of valuable content that even casual fans love.

Anyway, before I launch into an assault on streaming platforms' misjudgment, I want to talk about how an author could "hack" the audio commentary process for their books.

I took part in a Kickstarter campaign this year that successfully funded. It was a short story anthology that I contributed to. One of the stretch goals was audio commentary. The anthology editor told me to pick at least three places in the short story where I could expound on what inspired those sections, much like a director talks about a section in a movie commentary and how it inspired them or what went on behind the scenes.

To paraphrase his directions, he said, "Think of it as if the reader could tap the section in your story and listen to what inspired it."

That got me thinking about how I could commandeer this

idea for my books. It's really quite simple, and I'm surprised I didn't think of it sooner.

Here's how it would work: I could record high-quality audio commentary and host it on a website with links that do not change. I could then link it to text that inspired the commentary. If the reader wants to hear it, they can simply tap on the link. Or, to make this a little less obtrusive, I could hide the link in a footnote and set the expectation on the copyright page and the author's note so that the reader can tap the footnotes to listen to the commentary.

For paperback readers, I could simply print a QR code in the back of the book that takes them to a playlist with commentary. I would just need to be intentional about naming the files and announcing the chapter and section at the beginning of the recordings so that readers know where they are.

Furthermore, I could release a limited edition or special edition of my books with this feature enabled, in addition to other things like AI art inspired by the series, a video interview with me talking about the book, and other bonuses. Hell, this is the kind of content you could put in an omnibus. I always struggle when thinking about what to add to those to make the higher price point more attractive. This would be a great way to get people to buy omnibuses.

The only problem is figuring out the hosting situation. I think I could use a service like Google Drive or Dropbox, but I would have to look at the fine print. It's one thing if you're selling a few copies of your novel here and there; it's another thing entirely if your book becomes a bestseller. That would drive traffic to your files, and a hosting service might not like that. However you addressed this issue, you would need to ensure without a doubt that readers could access the files at all times and that there would be no surprises. Perhaps a podcast hosting provider such as Libsyn would be a smart way to host this content safely and permanently, but the downside is that you would have to pay for it, which is a non-starter if you are not selling that many books.

And, of course, there is the untapped functionality of EPUB 3, something I'd like to explore soon.

This is the most sophisticated way around the audio commentary problem I can think of. As I wrote this chapter, I found myself getting very excited about the prospects of this workaround.

WRITING WHILE TRAVELING

In a previous chapter, I discussed my struggles with writing while my wife was out of town. Several weeks later, we took a family trip to Chicago. I was back to my regular productivity routine, hitting and exceeding my quota on most days.

Now, suddenly, I was faced with a new challenge: how could I continue being productive while on the road? I feel like I'm always asking this question, and it feels like the answer changes every time I address it. What made this particular trip unique is that:

1. My surplus was anemic due to the productivity downturn I described in a previous chapter.
2. I had a lot more control over what to write, and I had a unique opportunity to choose my project before the trip because I was writing primarily short stories and nonfiction. This would have been a completely different chapter if I had been in the middle of a novel (or wanted to start one).

We left on Thursday and came home on Sunday. That

meant I needed to write a total of 11,000 words while on the road, or I needed to make up for any lost words before I left or when I returned.

First, I built up my surplus as high as possible between Sunday and Wednesday. Fortunately, I left for Chicago with a surplus for the week. That meant I started the trip slightly ahead of schedule and could afford to slip a little in case I didn't hit my quota on some days.

Next, I chose a nonfiction book as my primary project while on the road. While I didn't like that too much because I wanted to focus on fiction, nonfiction is a lot easier to write and requires less friction to get started. Therefore, I could achieve higher word counts on the days I traveled simply by virtue of writing nonfiction. That was a beautiful thing.

I also had another nonfiction book in reserve in case I needed to divert words to it, and, if I wrote an exceptional amount, I also had a fiction short story teed up to start, but if I started the short story, I made sure that I didn't start it until at least Sunday morning. This way, I wouldn't start the story and have to stop it in the middle, like I did with my productivity downturn. If there's anything I've learned, it's that if you start a story, your primary goal should be to finish it as soon as possible with no delays. Otherwise, finishing the story takes twice as long and twice as much effort.

Next, I used every opportunity to write on my phone. My wife and I alternated driving, and the drive from Des Moines to Chicago is approximately five hours. I spent my two and a half hours in the passenger seat writing. I did this even though it only amounted to a few hundred words both ways. When you're on the road, a few hundred words goes a long way.

Next, I made sure that my email inbox was at zero before I left. I find that when I zero out my inbox, the "zero effect" lasts for approximately two days before emails with action items start rolling in. What's in your email inbox is what's on your mind. Since there was nothing in my email inbox, I could focus on writing.

I also brought my voice recorder with me and used some down time in the evenings to take a walk and dictate.

Lastly, I made sure to rest when I got home. I didn't immediately run down to my writing computer even though I had a deficit. By getting rest, I was able to take a long nap and wake up refreshed. This helped me make a dent in my deficit, and I ultimately met my quota for the week even though I spent more than half of it away from home.

So, that's what it's like to write while traveling when you want to achieve one million words per year.

SELF-SUFFICIENT SELF-PUBLISHING

As I did my planning for 2023, I realized that I was moving toward a destination that I hadn't yet been able to articulate for myself. As I looked at my accomplishments for the last three years and I now look ahead to the next few years, I realized that I am moving toward something that I call "self-sufficient self-publishing."

I define self-sufficient self-publishing as follows: the ability to run a profitable publishing business without overreliance on others.

As the global economy heads into an economic downturn and the future looks uncertain, this will be more important than ever. It is the answer to continuing to publish on your terms without undue financial stress. In other words, it is the ultimate freedom as an author and artist.

I believe it's critically important to build a publishing business that runs itself. I've discussed ad nauseum my commitment to technology and data to make that happen, but there is much more to it than that.

Creativity

As writers, we often feel that we need the opinions and validation of others. We frequently tie our self-worth to the performance of our books, but that is a terrible idea. Before even going into some of the more mechanical aspects of self-sufficient self-publishing, I want to stress that one must also become emotionally self-sufficient with their writing. They must not succumb to self-doubt, comparisonitis, and unnecessary anxiety. Otherwise, self-sufficient self-publishing will never become a reality because they will be too dependent emotionally on others.

This means doing the emotional work to fortify your mind, body, and spirit so that you can continue writing no matter what happens in your life. Life happens to us all, but a writer is someone who writes, even when life strikes.

Writing Books

Learning how to write quality stories as quickly as possible is a career-defining trait for any writer. The more you publish, the more potential money you will make. The math of publishing is simple enough, but many people choose to play checkers when the real game is chess. It's not about quantity versus quality. It's about quality *and* quantity. That's the challenge, and the writer who can figure that out will tap into a bonanza.

Of course, this requires the convergence of craft, marketing, and business, but I believe that it is possible. I see no reason why it can't be. I see more people giving excuses about why they can't achieve world-class quality instead of actually figuring out if there is a way for them to achieve both. I believe we should change the conversation and the lens through which we look at what it means to be a writer.

What if you could publish the books in your mind quicker? How many books would that be? What if you did the very best you could on all those stories? What if readers proved they didn't care about quantity versus quality, and they--this never happens--they actually got mad at you because you had too many books?

I'd call that a good problem. Readers love challenges like that, especially when you operate at a consistent quality.

Editing Your Books

Here's where the rubber meets the road. To publish a book, you need to have it edited. An editor is someone whom you rely on to publish a book.

At a minimum, you must ensure that you always have access to an editor, no matter what happens. If you must wait many months to get on an editor's calendar, then you are hamstringing your writing output.

Therefore, you owe it to yourself to learn how to create manuscripts that are as clean as possible to reduce your editing costs. Fortunately, editors are easy to find, easy to work with, and generally don't have long waits, but if that were ever to change--that's what you need to be thinking about.

Economic times change. Just because you can find an editor easy today doesn't mean that you will be able to find one easily tomorrow. All I'm proposing is that you learn how to exercise sanity in these moments of mania. That sanity comes from long-term thinking, smart planning, and prudent decision-making.

For example, if my current editor became unavailable temporarily or permanently, I would take the following steps:

- If possible, I would look to editors I've worked with in the past to see if they are available.
- If my previous editors are unavailable within my price range, I will look for another editor on the

common channels where authors find editors like Reedsy, Upwork, and word of mouth.

If there were a disaster and I could not find the right person, I would call the head of the English department at my alma mater, tell them to send me their brightest English major, and I would pay them a fair fee to read my manuscripts and comment on them. I would instruct them to look for basic spelling and grammar errors. Nothing more, nothing less. Sure, this person wouldn't be a professional, but there are tens of thousands of college students out there who need money and experience. Even with liberal arts programs in shambles, I am confident I would have no problem finding someone to work on my books.

If such a scenario were to occur, and I had to rely on a college student for editing, then the burden of ensuring clean manuscripts would especially be on me. Therefore, it would be in my best interest to ensure that my manuscripts are as error-free as possible before they ever went to the college student.

Why not do that now, when times are good? Clean manuscripts are clean manuscripts, and clean manuscripts are a smart idea no matter who you are as a writer. This is why I have spent so much time implementing automation and technology into my workflow to clean up my text as much as possible. It's why I spent so much time on my dictation macros, because they are the clearest path to cleanliness.

But there's also another snake in the grass here that I need to be wary of: Dragon software. As I wrote in a previous chapter, Microsoft acquired Nuance Software. As I write this chapter, the tech industry is going through an economic bust, with tens of thousands of layoffs that look to be surpassing the dotcom boom in the years 2000 and 2001. The optimist in me says that everything will work out and I will continue to be able to use

Dragon as I do today; the pessimist in me says that there are some red lights flashing that I need to pay attention to:

- For Mac users, the only way to run Dragon is on a virtual machine using Parallels or Bootcamp. The new Apple Silicon chips do not support virtual machines, so while Parallels works on Apple Silicon Macs, it doesn't work well right now. That may not ever change due to the direction Apple is headed. Therefore, assuming that Dragon will continue working on a Windows virtual machine is not a safe bet.
- When companies get acquired, their products get retired. If Microsoft integrates the Dragon technology into its Microsoft Office platform, it will change. Some of those changes will be positive, and some of them will be negative, but there will always be an impact. Sometimes users come out ahead; most often, they do not.
- If Dragon became unavailable tomorrow, there would be no viable alternatives except for Whisper. But only the most tech-savvy people can use Whisper right now.

So why not learn how to use Whisper now? Why not reduce my dependence on Dragon so that I won't be nearly as impacted when the fateful day comes and Microsoft makes a product deprecation announcement?

Many authors use Dragon for dictation and transcription; if it went away tomorrow, there would be mania.

Book Cover Design

Perhaps the biggest expense that authors have is book cover design. I've talked about my gripes with book cover designers enough that I don't need to rehash them here. Suffice it to say that we rely on cover designers too much. In fact, we rely on them so much that we are at their whims.

Self-sufficient self-publishing means you can create high-quality, professional covers without needing a cover designer. Or, if you need a cover designer, you don't need them as often.

Here's the doomsday scenario: due to a massive economic downturn or a change in the industry, cover designers become unavailable, and the shortage is even worse than it is now, driving the rates way up. New authors will be priced out of publishing entirely, and mid-list authors will have to cut their production because they cannot afford to publish at the same pace they are used to. Only the most affluent authors will be able to afford rapid-release publishing. That's a scary landscape. Both authors *and* readers lose.

A self-sufficient self-publisher, while they may not be among the most affluent, would not be impacted at all by a cover designer shortage because they can design their own covers. They can do more with less. So, though a self-sufficient publisher may not be affluent, they would have more opportunities to grab market share and readers because everyone else won't publish nearly as much.

So, why not start learning cover design now?

Bringing It All Together

A self-sufficient self-publisher can continue writing and publishing rain or shine because:

- They do not rely emotionally on the opinions of others and therefore work independently.

- They publish independently.
- The methods by which they work are independent and not overly reliant on industry changes or the whims of tech giants.
- They produce manuscripts that are so clean that they could technically publish them without editing.
- They create their own covers or pay significantly less than others to get better results.
- Their profit margins are astronomically higher compared to other authors with similar experience levels, and they reinvest their profit back into the business in good times so that they can thrive in hard times when everyone else is suffering.

As I did my planning, that's what I realized I was heading toward—self-sufficient self-publishing. I'm fortunate enough that my writing business is profitable, but even if it weren't, I could continue publishing at the same pace and building my platform. In other words, I will keep charging forward as long and as fast as possible, no matter what is happening around me. That's critical.

MY THOUGHTS ON THE METAVERSE

I have been studying virtual reality and augmented reality a lot this quarter after I experienced what they can do. The technology has come a long way over the last few years, and people are exhibiting shortsighted behavior when it comes to the metaverse.

Say what you want about virtual reality. Yes, the headsets look gimmicky and inconvenient to wear for long periods. However, virtual reality *headsets* were never the point. The point was always augmented reality. Today's headsets are no different from the chunky cathode ray tube computer monitors that existed in the 1990s and early 2000s. It's the same thing. The technology will eventually become more like glasses, and when it does, it will take off. Most people are too shortsighted to understand this.

Also, say what you want about Mark Zuckerberg. I have my gripes with him, and I'm no fan of Facebook. However, I do believe his vision is clear, and it is correct.

We should also acknowledge another fact: Zuckerberg was simply the first to recognize where society is going, and because he is one of the richest men in the world, he has a disproportionate influence on where we will go. I have some problems with that, as I am not someone who is going to simp to the billionaire class. I'm under no illusions about the seemingly altruistic initiatives of billionaires, but I am also not in the realm of politics or policymaking, and, because the future is what it is, we've all got to survive as best we can. That means thinking ahead and adapting to new technology and working methods. Otherwise, we will be left behind. This is a particular danger for writers, for whom developers may not support as well as other professions and an increasingly technological future where people will need to pay for services and subscriptions.

I've said for a while that the future will be what we make it, and no one will do anything for us; if we want something, we have to be the stewards of our fates. And if the world is headed toward a metaverse, we must learn how to make it work for us rather than focusing on things we don't like and resisting the technology. You can see how well that worked out for people who decried the Internet and smartphones. Hint: it didn't work out so well.

I have my problems with the metaverse too. I've read *Snow Crash* and *Ready Player One* like everyone else, and if Mark Zuckerberg ever asked me for constructive criticism, I would tell him that his biggest problem when he unveiled his vision of the metaverse is that he didn't address these books, and that he didn't explain that he was trying to create positive versions of the technology detailed in those books. The result was that people subconsciously assumed that Zuckerberg was trying to take us to a bleak, dismal reality where we have no agency or cause for optimism. I don't think that's what Zuckerberg had in mind.

Instead, the headlines around Meta's metaverse were negative due to this association.

Whether Zuckerberg realizes his vision or not, the metaverse will be here to stay.

The core philosophy of the metaverse, virtual reality, and augmented reality seems to be this: let's take everything that people do in real life and make it better in the metaverse. That's where the use cases are right now.

For example, if you work from home using a tiny little laptop, why not use virtual or augmented reality to spawn as many screens as you need? Instead of two-dimensional Zoom calls, why not meet your colleagues in a realistic 3D work room where you have a full-body avatar that tracks your eye and facial expressions? This way, you can talk and interact with your colleagues as if you were in the same room, even though you may be halfway around the world. Sure, it's not the real thing, but it's the closest we can get to human interaction. Avatars look cartoonish right now, but in a few years, you will be able to create an avatar of your real body.

For gaming, why not become the character you're playing? The metaverse takes the term "first-person shooter" to a whole new level. The future of video games is in the first-person. (This saddens me because I never was a first-person videogame kind of guy. I prefer third-person experiences, but how cool would it be to play a game like *Final Fantasy* where *you* are the protagonist?)

If you want to hang out with friends who don't live near you, why not spawn your avatars in a virtual environment so that you can do things like go to the movies, go bowling, sit around and chat while having a coffee, and so on? Otherwise, you'd have to travel to get to them.

Need to learn how to drive? Do it with augmented reality. How about archery? Or shooting a gun? Or any other tactile function where it may not always be possible to physically attend?

The future of events is virtual as well. I predict that in the very near future, I will be conducting speaking engagements as an avatar to participants who reside in a virtual room. They will be able to ask me questions, and I will be able to interact with them as if we were in the same room.

The future of schools is also virtual. Especially colleges. Think about it. College is so damn expensive these days. Instead of flying halfway across the country to a school where you have to pay excessive room and board, many students can simply be "digital commuters." The colleges of the future may not even have a single real estate footprint. Sure, nothing beats the actual experience of living in a dormitory, but legacy colleges where you attend physically will probably be bastions of the rich.

I even think there is a use case for digital sports. With special equipment and headsets, it's not out of the realm of possibility that we could have something like a virtual Olympics.

And we haven't even gotten to augmented reality yet.

Imagine walking down the street and seeing your text messages pop up in your peripheral vision. Or, as already exists, imagine walking down the street and seeing turn-by-turn directions appear in front of you.

Anyway, I can see the future of the metaverse very clearly, and I have decided to become an early adopter. The term "writer of the future" will encompass the metaverse. Here are some use cases across every phase of publishing that I think the metaverse could potentially touch, allowing us to do our best work faster and more efficiently.

Creativity. With a pair of augmented glasses, imagine being inspired in the moment and turning your glasses to record mode (we will ignore the potential problems that this could cause, as it did with Google Glass in the mid-2010s). Let's say you walk into a bakery that inspires you. Record the experience exactly as you see it through your own eyes, and you can narrate it as well, as if you were recording it with a high-quality DSLR. The augmented glasses could potentially scan the entire area, and you could replay the event virtually, going back to review particular spots of the recording that you want to remember. What did that painting on the north wall look like again? What was the music playing over the loudspeakers when you entered? What was the guy at the front counter bellyaching about? This would take the term "replay" to a whole new level.

When you want to capture ideas today, you do it in two dimensions. In the future, you will be able to capture your ideas in three dimensions.

Also, you will be able to create your own custom digital workrooms. Let's say that you live in a tiny studio apartment, and you don't really have a writing space, so to speak. No problem. You can design (or hire someone to design) the perfect writing space. It would be your home away from home, especially if you don't want to spend a ton of money on coffee at coffee shops or if your writing space just isn't that pleasant to look at in the first place.

And it's not just a visual trick. You could also have a whiteboard that syncs wirelessly with your digital notebook software, so you could draw, take notes, outline your novel, and so much more without needing paper for physical space.

For the right people, this will be a game changer. I bet that there would even be solutions for people who are neurodivergent or have disabilities. These peaceful, serene writing spaces might be the best way for them to work.

Writing And Editing. This is a tougher vision because I'm not quite sure how it will shake out, but I do think that the way we write will change.

Writing is writing, and editing is editing, and I don't think the fundamental activities of each will change that dramatically. I think we will be able to do more faster with augmented reality.

As you're writing and you come across the need to research something, your virtual environment would change. The lights in the room would come back on, multiple screens would return--one with a web browser, maybe one with a dictionary--and you would be free to carry on your research until it's time to start writing again, in which case the room will go into a do not disturb mode again. When you're editing, the words could become the room, with your entire manuscript wrapped around you like a big circle. You could walk between the pages, and augmented reality would make the typos lift off the page so you could see them more easily. Combined with artificial intelligence, you could simply touch a section, speak to edit it, and watch the words magically transform before your very eyes.

Formatting. When it's time to format your book, you can use a previewer to hold a sample device in your hands and test out the e-book version. Imagine holding an actual e-reader, testing the operating system, and proofing your book. This could work the same way with paperbacks.

Marketing. Marketing is so two-dimensional these days. When it's time for you to market your books with virtual reality, you will be able to interact with your readers through your avatar. After all, readers buy from authors they know, like, and trust; if they have met your avatar and like you, they will be more likely to look you up in the future.

Imagine doing book readings, author interviews, and even speaking engagements and writing conferences as a virtual avatar in a virtual convention center.

This could also be interesting with augmented reality. If you attend an in-person event and meet people, imagine information bars that pop up over their heads. Let's say you're getting coffee at a concession station, and you start a conversation with a fellow author you've never met before. In theory, both of you could opt into an application where you put in your information, such as the types of books you write, where you live, and other interests that could be great icebreakers. The information bar would display the information that is most relevant to your conversation. You would skip the small talk and jump into real conversation. For example, your coffee mate might also write in the same subgenre as science fiction as you do. You might even see the cover of their latest book. In plain reality, you could be standing next to a bestseller and not even know it. In augmented reality, you'll never be caught off-guard.

Imagine a system where people can opt into public profiles, and when someone passes you on the street, you get their information. Yes, I know this is a little big brother-ish, but I'm looking at the optimistic side of things. In this fashion, augmented reality could help people make deeper and more meaningful connections in a world where we seem to be losing the ability to do that.

New Experiences. While I'm not a big fan of this use case, it's not out of the realm of possibility that authors could partner with developers to create their own virtual reality experiences. Mystery authors will have an amazing opportunity here. Imagine a series of mystery books where you are the protagonist and must solve a murder. In your virtual avatar, you will traverse a city and visit all sorts of locales to solve that murder. You might even have to find a bad guy or two. Good God, would this make for amazing virtual reality experiences, especially if the genesis is a best-selling series of books!

Science fiction and fantasy authors will have a great time with this too because they can create entire worlds, new races of characters, and all sorts of quests and missions that readers can go on and feel like they are truly in an immersive experience.

Nonfiction authors can also benefit from this. Imagine selling access to a course or service that you attend virtually. For example, if I'm a nutritionist, I could hold a seminar with a thousand people in a packed virtual auditorium and teach a class there—no more 2D Zoom calls. The same is true with anyone who offers a consulting service.

Those are just a few use cases I can think of that could positively impact writers. As I said, I'm excited about the future. It may not happen as soon as we want, but it can also happen sooner than anyone expected. Regardless, I'll be prepared, and I'll be right out front.

MASTERING THE FUNDAMENTALS

In 2021, I wrote that 2022 was the final year to get my fundamentals right. Here's why I wrote that.

Given the impending future that is on the way (and in some respects, here now), it'd be awfully easy to want to protect the publishing status quo. There's something simple and quaint about writing books, uploading them, doing some marketing, and enjoying the benefit of your hard work. Why mess around with blockchains, AI, Web 3.0, and other technology that has a deep learning curve and requires a skill set many authors currently do not have?

That's what I think will happen. It's human nature. Therefore, I must resist that nature and try to see the potential in any new technology despite criticisms, however valid those criticisms are.

I believe 2022 is the last full year to get my fundamentals in order. Change is coming, and I want to be ready when it arrives so I can take advantage of it...repeatedly. When December 31st, 2022 arrives, I will stand ready to finally become the writer of the future—the result of several years of planning.

Wow, was I right. It's December 26, 2022 as I write this, and I'm five days away from that deadline.

What fundamentals did I work on?

Sound business fundamentals and a good tax strategy. I had a profitable writing year and am set up to do quite well with my taxes. Check.

Being a writing machine, writing more books than the average author per year with less effort. This year, I wrote 12 books and published 10.

Creating manuscripts with fewer errors than the average author's. Based on my data, my average copy-edits for my novels this year were 1 edit per 673 words. In 2018, my average was 1 edit per 346 words. I nearly doubled my quality in this area, and I continue to improve.

Turning the art of publishing into a science by creating high-quality, well-packaged books on day one. With my final book this year, *Be a Writing Machine* 2, I released the e-book, trade paperback, large print, and audiobook editions on day one. That's the first time I've succeeded in accomplishing this task, and I now have the tools and workflow to do this with every book I publish. Not every book will get all editions, but the point stands.

Maximized distribution, meaning the books are available to buy everywhere humanly possible. This is true of my catalog now that I am finally distributing it through IngramSpark.

Maximized formats, meaning the books are available in as many formats as I can manage. Check.

A reliable and sizable community of people willing to buy my books on day one. Check.

A good, up-to-date website that gets the right

book to the right reader at the right time. Semi-check, though I plan to create a new website sometime in the next one to two years.

The ability to track expenses using automation. Check.

The ability to track book sales using automation. Check.

The ability to use data to make informed decisions about the business. I've talked about this enough.

Reducing costs wherever possible to keep the business lean and ready for anything. I've learned to do my own covers, which will go a long way toward satisfying this fundamental.

Supreme organization skills. Check.

An estate plan that takes care of my family. Check, evidenced by writing *The Author Estate Handbook* and *The Author Heir Handbook.*

Chaining all of these elements together with technology to increase my efficiency and deliver more value to my readers. Check.

In short, I have delivered on the major fundamentals of being an author. By improving my quality and quantity, production workflow, and utilizing data and technology, I am extremely well-positioned to take advantage of everything that 2023 has to offer.

With the rise of AI art, new chatbot and AI writing technology, rising cover art costs, and so much more, I feel good about navigating this new shifting landscape we're entering. Whether I succeed or not is another story, but at least little will catch me by surprise.

Since I am no longer focused on the fundamentals, the theme for next year is this: taking advantage of hidden opportunities that others are missing because they are stuck in the status quo. I do not expect these opportunities to bear fruit in 2023 or even 2024, but they will lay the groundwork for long-term advantages. So, in other words, the things I will be doing may look like failures. Some will be, but the wins will be big wins.

Here's to 2023.

Q4 PROGRESS REPORT

2022 is now over. It was a good year but not a great year. That said, I made a ton of progress toward my goals.

BECOME A WORLD-CLASS CONTENT CREATOR

To achieve my goal of becoming a world-class content creator, I will focus on the following tactical priorities:

- Demonstrate a commitment to learning the craft of storytelling and teaching
- Demonstrate a commitment to outstanding quality AND quantity

Examples of day-to-day activities that will help me carry out my tactical priorities include:

- Keep learning through online courses and workshops taught by professional writers who are further down the path I want to write
- Reading
- Developing mentorships
- Finding new ways to increase my daily word counts
- Mastering different writing methods
- Documenting my process of becoming a successful writer in the *Indie Author Confidential* series
- Cleaning up my platform to ensure a consistent quality reader experience

What did I do to become a world-class content creator during Q4 2022?

1. I deepened the relationship with my mentor acquired in Q3.
2. I have read (and studied the craft in) 35 books.
3. I am still on track to publish 100 books by end of 2023.

BECOME A TECHNOLOGY AND DATA-DRIVEN WRITER

To achieve my goal of becoming a technology and data-driven writer, I will focus on the following tactical priorities:

- Use technology to make the business more efficient
- Use data to get insights

Examples of day-to-day activities that will help me carry out my tactical priorities include:

- Developing a tax plan

- Developing an estate plan assisted with technology
- Learning how to design my own covers
- Hiring a personal assistant for small tasks where it makes sense
- Developing a metadata database for my work
- Improving my readers' experience on my website
- Implementing direct sales for my fiction

What did I do to become a more technology and data-driven writer during Q4 2022?

1. I began ramping up my testing of AI apps to improve my workflow and processes.
2. I began learning how to design my own book covers.

HIGHLIGHTS

There were many highlights this year, but here are a few.

Become a World-Class Content Creator:

- I ended the year with 81 books published. While reaching 100 will be a stretch, it's not impossible.
- I exploded my dictation word counts with voice recorder dictation.
- I started writing short fiction again, sending my work out to magazines.
- I am now officially an international public speaker.

Become a Technology and Data-Driven Writer:

- I produced cleaner manuscripts with enhancements to my dictation macros.
- I created a sophisticated word count tracker.
- I upgraded my microphone and audio setup, resulting in higher quality video and audio for my YouTube channel and media interviews.

Become the Writer of the Future:

- I branched into AI audio, publishing my first titles in the medium.
- I began exploring how to leverage AI to transform my writing career.

As I said, this was a challenging year. My wife received a devastating long COVID diagnosis, and I had to have a major surgery this year. Those things definitely set me back, but I still have a lot to show for this year.

MY 2023 STRATEGIC PRIORITIES

2022 gave me clarity.

2020 was about survival and staying focused. 2021 was about building on success. I started 2022 with the aim of creating stability and a new normal. That happened in some respects, but in others, I got what I wished for in unexpected ways.

To say that my life was upended in 2022 is an understatement. Yet it taught me a lot about resilience, and it made me grateful.

You see, I've spent so much time automating and focusing on the things that matter. Even though 2022 wasn't as great as I hoped, I was still able to keep producing books and make record profit—all while facing tough personal issues.

If I hadn't spent the last ten years leading up to this year, it could have been devastating for me. But it wasn't, and I live to write another day.

Last year, I reduced my number of strategic priorities from five to three. That worked very well.

In 2023, I will maintain my three strategic priorities, but I will be changing how much time I allocate to them. Currently, I spend equal time on content creation, technology and data, and looking forward. In 2023, I will be reallocating my time so that 50 of my time is spent looking forward and the remaining time is divided between content creation and technology and data.

Why?

I still need to publish 100 books of course, but that is secondary to making a big pivot. As I wrote last year, I believe that 2022 is the last year to get my fundamentals right because things are changing in a big way. I need to be prepared to pivot in 2023, and to do that, I have to spend a significant amount of time learning new skills, particularly with AI. I anticipate that my first half of 2023 will be very quiet production-wise. That's okay because I'll make up for it with the knowledge I'll learn.

2023 is about leaning into the paradigm shift that's coming. I'm as ready as I will ever be. I'm extremely prolific, have a profitable writing business, and have made key investments that are beginning to pay off. Now it's time to figure out what's next: what the future of writing will look like.

I don't know what 2023 will have in store for me, but I'm looking forward to finding out.

CAN YOU KEEP A SECRET?

If you liked the ideas in this book, check out the rest of the volumes in the series at www.authorlevelup.com/confidential.

MEET M.L. RONN

Science fiction and fantasy on the wild side!

M.L. Ronn (Michael La Ronn) is the author of many science fiction and fantasy novels including *The Good Necromancer*, *Android X,* and *The Last Dragon Lord* series.

In 2012, a life-threatening illness made him realize that storytelling was his #1 passion. He's devoted his life to writing ever since, making up whatever story makes him fall out of his chair laughing the hardest. Every day.

Learn more about Michael
www.authorlevelup.com (for writers)
www.michaellaronn.com (fiction)

MORE BOOKS BY M.L. RONN

Books for Writers

Indie Author Confidential (Series)
    How to Write Your First Novel
    Be a Writing Machine
    Mental Models for Writers
    The Indie Writer's Encyclopedia
    The Indie Author Atlas
    The Indie Author Bestiary
    The Reader's Bill of Rights
    The Self-Publishing Compendium
    150 Self-Publishing Questions Answered
    Authors, Steal This Book
    The Indie Author Strategy Guide
    How to Dictate a Book
    Advanced Author Editing
    Keep Your Books Selling
    The Author Estate Handbook
    The Author Heir Handbook

Interactive Fiction: How to Engage Readers and Push the Boundaries of Story Telling

Indie Poet Rock Star

Indie Poet Formatting

2016 Indie Author State of the Union

More Books for Writers:

www.authorlevelup.com/books

Fiction:

www.michaellaronn.com/books